Python for Data Science:
Zero to Hero

Python for Data Science: Zero to Hero

Copyright © 2023 by Teo Kok Keong

Introduction

Welcome to "Python for Data Science: Zero to Hero"!

We're thrilled that you've embarked on this transformative journey to unlock the incredible world of data science using Python. Over the next 10 days, you will embark on an exciting adventure that will take you from being a complete beginner to a confident data science practitioner.

Python, a versatile and powerful programming language, is your gateway to exploring and analyzing data, making informed decisions, and creating data-driven solutions. Whether you're pursuing a career in data science, enhancing your analytical skills, or simply curious about the possibilities, this course is designed to empower you with the knowledge and practical skills you need.

Each day of this course is carefully crafted to provide you with step-by-step guidance, hands-on exercises, and a supportive learning environment. The activities spanning a period of ten days are outlined in Table 1 and 2 for your reference

Day	Topic	Reading Assignment	Hands-on exercises
1	Python Essential	Introduction to Python	• Installing Python and IDEs • Write your first Python script • Variables, data types, and basic operations
2	Control Structures	Introduction to Control Structures	• Selection Logic (if, elif, else) • Repeat-While Structure(for and while)
3	Functions and Modules	Understanding functions	• Parameters, arguments, and return values •
4	Working with Data	Introduction to data structures (lists, tuples, dictionaries)	• Manipulating data structures • manipulation • slicing, indexing • data manipulation exercises
5	Data Analysis with Pandas	Introduction to Pandas data frames, Data cleaning and preprocessing	• Loading and exploring datasets • Selecting and filtering data •

Table1 Day 1-5 Activities

Day	Topic	Reading Assignment	Hands-on exercises
6	Data Visualization with Matplotlib and Seaborn	Introduction to data visualization	• basic plots (line, bar, scatter) • bar chart
7	Statistics for Data Science	• Descriptive statistics (mean, median, mode) • Measures of variability (variance, standard deviation) • Probability distributions (normal, binomial) • Introduction to hypothesis testing	Descriptive statistical exercise Hypothesis testing and etc
8	Machine Learning Basics	• Introduction to machine learning • Types of machine learning (supervised, unsupervised) • Model evaluation and validation	Building a simple linear regression model
9	Data Science Projects	• Overview of real-world data science projects	Exploratory Data Analysis (EDA) for a Retail Store
10	Advanced Topics and Beyond	• Advanced data science topics (deep learning, NLP, etc.)	•

Table2 Day 6-10 Activities

You'll learn to manipulate data, visualize insights, and even build machine learning models. By the end of this journey, you'll have the confidence to tackle real-world data challenges and take your first steps toward becoming a data science hero.

Remember, learning is a journey, and we're here to support you every step of the way. So, let's dive in and embark on this exhilarating adventure together. Get ready to transform from zero to hero in the exciting realm of Python for Data Science!

Please follow **Python for Data Science: Zero to Hero in 10 Days FB page** to access all the exercises code an support from the Author. FB page link https://www.facebook.com/pythonzero2hero

All the code listed in this book will be freely available in Github. The link will be provided in the **Python for Data Science: Zero to Hero in 10 Days FB page.**

Happy learning!

Sincerely,
Teo Kok Keong

Day1: Python Essential

Day1: Python Essential

Introduction to Python

Python is a versatile and widely used programming language known for its simplicity, readability, and power. Whether you're a complete beginner or an experienced programmer, Python is an excellent choice for a wide range of applications, and it's particularly well-suited for data science.

Key Features of Python

Readable and Understandable: Python's syntax is designed to be straightforward and easy to read, making it an ideal language for beginners. Code is organized through indentation, which enforces a clean and consistent structure.

Cross-Platform Compatibility: Python is cross-platform, meaning you can write code on one operating system (e.g., Windows) and run it on another (e.g., Linux or macOS) with little to no modification. This versatility simplifies software development and collaboration.

Rich Ecosystem: Python boasts a vast ecosystem of libraries and frameworks for various domains, from web development to scientific computing. In data science, libraries like NumPy, Pandas, Matplotlib, Seaborn, and scikit-learn are indispensable tools.

Interactivity: Python supports interactive coding through environments like Jupyter Notebooks, which allow you to execute code step by step and visualize results immediately. This interactivity is especially valuable for data analysis and experimentation.

Community Support: Python has a large and active community of developers and enthusiasts who contribute to its growth. This community-driven approach ensures that Python remains up-to-date, secure, and well-documented.

Versatility: Python is not limited to a specific domain. You can use it for web development, automation, scientific computing, artificial intelligence, machine learning, and, of course, data science. Its versatility makes it a valuable skill in various industries.

Python in Data Science

Python has emerged as the predominant programming language for data science and analytics. Its widespread adoption can be attributed to its simplicity, versatility, and a rich ecosystem of libraries that cater to every facet of data analysis and machine learning.

At its core, Python's simplicity and readability make it an excellent choice for data science beginners and experts alike. The language is designed with a clean and straightforward syntax that is easy to understand, reducing the learning curve for those entering the field of data science. This characteristic makes Python accessible to a broad audience, including scientists, engineers, and statisticians, who may not have a deep background in programming.

One of Python's standout strengths in the realm of data science is its vast library support. Libraries like Pandas, NumPy, and SciPy provide a comprehensive toolkit for data manipulation, numerical computing, and scientific computing, respectively. Pandas, in particular, has become synonymous with data wrangling, allowing data scientists to efficiently clean, transform, and analyze data with ease. NumPy and SciPy provide the building blocks for performing complex mathematical and scientific operations, making Python suitable for a wide range of data-related tasks.

When it comes to data visualization, Python doesn't disappoint. Libraries like Matplotlib and Seaborn offer powerful tools for creating informative and visually appealing charts, graphs, and plots. Whether you need to create a simple bar chart or a complex heat map, Python's visualization libraries provide the flexibility and customization options to suit your needs. Additionally, libraries like Plotly and Bokeh enable the creation of interactive visualizations that enhance data exploration and presentation.

Machine learning is another area where Python shines brightly. The scikit-learn library provides a robust framework for building and evaluating machine learning models. With scikit-learn, data scientists can easily apply various algorithms for tasks like classification, regression, clustering, and more. Python's machine learning ecosystem extends beyond scikit-learn, with specialized libraries like TensorFlow and PyTorch for deep learning tasks. This versatility allows data scientists to tackle a wide range of problems, from predictive analytics to natural language processing.

Python's data science community is highly active and collaborative. The Python Package Index (PyPI) hosts a vast collection of open-source packages and libraries contributed by developers and data scientists from around the world. This wealth of resources enables data scientists to leverage existing solutions and avoid reinventing the wheel, ultimately speeding up the development process.

The simplicity and versatility of Python make it an ideal choice for not only data scientists but also businesses looking to harness the power of data-driven insights. Many organizations have adopted Python as their primary language for data analytics and machine learning due to its ease of integration with existing systems, seamless deployment capabilities, and a large pool of Python developers available in the job market.

In conclusion, Python has rightfully earned its place as the go-to language for data science and analytics. Its simplicity, combined with an extensive library ecosystem that covers data manipulation, visualization, and machine learning, makes it the preferred choice for data scientists of all skill levels. Python's adaptability and vibrant community ensure that it will continue to play a central role in shaping the future of data science and analytics.

In this course, you will embark on a 10-day journey to learn Python for data science. You'll explore Python's fundamentals, control structures, functions, data manipulation, data analysis, visualization, statistics, machine learning, and more. By the end of this course, you'll have the skills and confidence to harness Python's full potential in the exciting world of data science.

So, let's dive into the world of Python and discover the endless possibilities it offers for data analysis, visualization, and machine learning. Get ready to unlock the power of Python for data science!

Hand-on: Installing Python and IDEs

To begin your journey in Python, you'll need to set up Python on your computer. Python can be easily installed, and there are various Integrated Development Environments (IDEs) available to make coding in Python more efficient. Here's how to get started:

Step 1: Installing Python

Download Python: Visit the official Python website at python.org and download the latest version of Python for your operating system (Windows, macOS, or Linux). Python 3.x is the recommended version.

Installation: Run the installer you downloaded. During the installation, make sure to check the box that says "Add Python X.X to PATH" (where X.X represents the Python version). This will make it easier to run Python from the command line.

Verify Installation: Open your computer's terminal or command prompt and type *python --version* or *python3 --version*. You should see the Python version you installed, confirming a successful installation as shown in the figure below.

```
■ Command Prompt          ×   +  ∨

Microsoft Windows [Version 10.0.22621.2283]
(c) Microsoft Corporation. All rights reserved.

C:\Users\teokk>python --version
Python 3.10.6

C:\Users\teokk>
```

Figure 1 confirming Python successfully installed

Step 2 Installation of pip

The PyPA recommended tool for installing Python packages is pip. This really useful for managing and installation python packages.

This is a Python script that uses some bootstrapping logic to install pip.
•   Download   the   script,   from https://bootstrap.pypa.io/get-pip.py.
•   Open a terminal/command prompt, cd to the folder containing the get-pip.py file and run *"python get-pip.py"*

We will use pip to install libraries later.

Step 2: Choosing an IDE (Integrated Development Environment)

While you can write Python code in a simple text editor, using an IDE can greatly enhance your coding experience. Here are a few popular Python IDEs:

Visual Studio Code (VSCode): A free and highly customizable code editor developed by Microsoft. It has a rich ecosystem of extensions that make it a great choice for Python development. In this book we will be using VSCode in all examples.
You could download the free community version from ttps://visualstudio.microsoft.com/downloads/

PyCharm: A powerful and feature-rich IDE specifically designed for Python development. It offers a free Community edition and a paid Professional edition.

Jupyter Notebook: If you're focused on data science, Jupyter Notebook is an interactive environment that's great for data exploration and analysis. You can install it separately or as part of the Anaconda distribution.

Hand-on: Write your first Python script

Once you have Python and an IDE installed, you're ready to start coding! Open your chosen IDE, create a new Python file, and you're on your way to mastering Python for data science. Enjoy your coding journey!

Launch VSCode by clicking on its icon in your applications or using the command-line if you're on a Unix-like system (Linux/macOS).

Create a New Python File in VSCode :
1. Click on "File" in the top-left corner.
2. Select "New File" to create a new, empty file.
3. Save the file with a `.py` extension, for example, `hello.py`. Choose a location on your computer where you want to save it.

Write the Python Code

Inside the `hello.py` file, type the following code:

```
print("Hello, World!")
```

This is a simple Python program that prints "Hello, World!" to the console.

Save the File:

Press `Ctrl + S` (Windows/Linux) or `Cmd + S` (macOS) to save the changes you made to the file.

Open Integrated Terminal:

In VSCode, click on "View" in the top menu and select "Terminal" to open the integrated terminal.

Run the Python Program

In the integrated terminal, navigate to the directory where you saved `hello.py` using the `cd` (change directory) command. For example, if you saved the file on your C:\myproject\day1. You navigate to your folder using the command:

Cd C:\myproject\day1

Then, you can run the Python program by typing:
python hello.py

Press `Enter`, and you should see the output "Hello, World!" displayed in the terminal as shown in the figure below.

| PROBLEMS | OUTPUT | DEBUG CONSOLE | TERMINAL | PORTS |

```
● PS C:\Users\teokk> cd C:\myproject\day1\
● PS C:\myproject\day1> python .\hello.py
  hello world
○ PS C:\myproject\day1> █
```

Figure 2 screenshot of terminal demo of running hello.py and its output

Hand-on: Variables, data types, and basic operations

Exercise 1: Variables and Data Types

Type the following code in a new python script using VSCode and saved in the folder of your choice as file name such as ex1.py and run the script in the terminal:

```
# 1. Create a variable called `name` and assign your name to it.
name = "John Doe"

# 2. Create a variable called `age` and assign your age to it (as an integer).
age = 30

# 3. Create a variable called `height` and assign your height in meters (as a float).
height = 1.75

# 4. Create a variable called `is_student` and assign `True` if you are a student, and `False` otherwise.
is_student = True

# 5. Print the values of these variables.
print("Name:", name)
print("Age:", age)
print("Height:", height)
print("Is Student:", is_student)
```

Note that whatever follows the tag # is considered a comment and will not be executable, but is included for human reading purposes only.

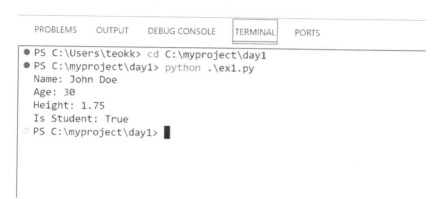

Figure 3 terminal output of running ex1.py

Exercise 2: Basic Operations

Type the following code in a new python script using VSCode and saved in the folder of your choice as file name such as ex2.py:

 # 1. Create a variable called `num1` and assign any integer value to it.
num1 = 20

 # 2. Create a variable called `num2` and assign another integer value to it.
num2 = 10

 # 3. Calculate the sum of `num1` and `num2` and store it in a variable called `sum_result`.
sum_result = num1 + num2

 # 4. Calculate the difference between `num1` and `num2` and store it in a variable called `difference_result`.
difference_result = num1 - num2

```
# 5. Calculate the product of `num1` and `num2` and store it in a
variable called `product_result`.
product_result = num1 * num2

# 6. Calculate the quotient (division) of `num1` by `num2` and store it
in a variable called `quotient_result`.
quotient_result = num1 / num2

# 7. Calculate the remainder of `num1` divided by `num2` and store
it in a variable called `remainder_result`.
remainder_result = num1 % num2

# 8. Print the results of all these operations.
print("Sum:", sum_result)
print("Difference:", difference_result)
print("Product:", product_result)
print("Quotient:", quotient_result)
print("Remainder:", remainder_result)
```

PROBLEMS	OUTPUT	DEBUG CONSOLE	TERMINAL	PORTS

```
● PS C:\Users\teokk> cd C:\myproject\day1
● PS C:\myproject\day1> python .\ex2.py
  Sum: 30
  Difference: 10
  Product: 200
  Quotient: 2.0
  Remainder: 0
○ PS C:\myproject\day1> █
```

Figure 4 terminal output of running ex2.py

Exercise 3: String Operations

Type the following code in a new python script using VSCode and saved in the folder of your choice as file name such as ex3.py:

```
# 1. Create a variable called `string1` and assign a string value to it.
string1 = "Hello"

# 2. Create another variable called `string2` and assign a different string value to it.
string2 = "World"

# 3. Concatenate `string1` and `string2` and store the result in a variable called `concatenated_string`.
concatenated_string = string1 + " " + string2

# 4. Print the `concatenated_string`.
print("Concatenated String:", concatenated_string)

# 5. Find the length of `concatenated_string` and store it in a variable called `string_length`.
string_length = len(concatenated_string)

# 6. Print the `string_length`.
print("String Length:", string_length)
```

```
PROBLEMS    OUTPUT    DEBUG CONSOLE    TERMINAL    PORTS

● PS C:\Users\teokk> cd C:\myproject\
● PS C:\myproject> cd day1
● PS C:\myproject\day1> python .\ex3.py
  Concatenated String: Hello World
  String Length: 11
○ PS C:\myproject\day1> █
```

Figure 5 terminal output of running ex3.py

Exercise 4: List Operations

Type the following code in a new python script using VSCode and saved in the folder of your choice as file name such as ex4.py:

```
# 1. Create a list called `fruits` and populate it with the names of five different fruits.
fruits = ["apple", "banana", "cherry", "date", "fig"]

# 2. Print the list of `fruits`.
print("Fruits:", fruits)

# 3. Add a new fruit to the list.
fruits.append("grape")

# 4. Remove one fruit from the list.
fruits.remove("cherry")

# 5. Print the updated list of `fruits`.
print("Updated Fruits:", fruits)
```

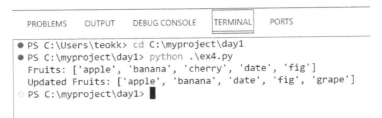

Figure 6 terminal output of running ex4.py

Exercise 5: Type Conversion

Type the following code in a new python script using VSCode and saved in the folder of your choice as file name such as ex5.py:

```
# 1. Create a variable called `number_string` and assign a numerical
string (e.g., "42") to it.
number_string = "42"

# 2. Convert `number_string` to an integer and store it in a variable
called `number_integer`.
number_integer = int(number_string)

# 3. Convert `number_string` to a float and store it in a variable
called `number_float`.
number_float = float(number_string)

# 4. Print the types and values of `number_string`, `number_integer`,
and `number_float`.
print("Type of number_string:", type(number_string), "Value:",
number_string)
print("Type of number_integer:", type(number_integer), "Value:",
number_integer)
print("Type of number_float:", type(number_float), "Value:",
number_float)
```

| PROBLEMS | OUTPUT | DEBUG CONSOLE | TERMINAL | PORTS |

```
● PS C:\Users\teokk> cd C:\myproject\day1
● PS C:\myproject\day1> python .\ex5.py
  Type of number_string: <class 'str'> Value: 42
  Type of number_integer: <class 'int'> Value: 42
  Type of number_float: <class 'float'> Value: 42.0
○ PS C:\myproject\day1> █
```

Figure 7 terminal output of running ex5.py

Recap for Day 1

Day 1 marked the beginning of our journey into the exciting world of data science and analytics. We started by recognizing Python as the undisputed champion in this field, owing to its simplicity and a vast ecosystem of libraries tailored for data manipulation, visualization, and machine learning.

Python's user-friendly syntax sets the stage for data scientists, welcoming both beginners and experts with open arms. Its readability and approachability are invaluable assets, making it an accessible language even for those without extensive programming backgrounds.

The day's focus was on Python's library landscape. We explored key libraries such as Pandas, NumPy, and SciPy, each serving a unique role in data analysis, numerical computing, and scientific operations. Pandas, in particular, stood out as the go-to tool for data manipulation, offering streamlined processes for cleaning, transforming, and exploring datasets.

Data visualization, another essential aspect of data science, found its champion in libraries like Matplotlib, Seaborn, Plotly, and Bokeh. These powerful tools allow data scientists to create informative and visually compelling charts and graphs, transforming raw data into meaningful insights.

Machine learning, a cornerstone of modern data science, was not left behind. The versatile scikit-learn library emerged as a formidable ally for building and evaluating machine learning models. We also touched upon specialized libraries like TensorFlow and PyTorch, paving the way for deep learning adventures in the future.

Python's vibrant data science community and the vast collection of open-source packages on the Python Package Index (PyPI) promise ongoing support and innovation. These resources are a testament to Python's adaptability and the collaborative spirit of the data science community.

As we conclude Day 1, we carry with us the foundational knowledge and tools necessary to embark on our data science journey. Python has proven itself as a reliable companion, ready to assist us in the exploration and analysis of data, as well as in the creation of meaningful visualizations and machine learning models.

With this strong start, we look forward to diving deeper into the intricacies of data science and analytics in the days to come, knowing that Python will remain our trusted ally in unraveling the mysteries hidden within data.

Day 2 Control Structures

Day 2 Control Structures

Reading Assignment: Control Structures

Control Structures are a way to specify the flow of control in programs. Using self-contained modules called logic or control structures can make algorithms or programs clearer and easier to understand. These structures analyze and determine the direction a program should take based on certain parameters or conditions. There are three main types of logic or flow of control:

Sequential logic, also known as sequential flow, follows a series of instructions given to the computer. Unless new instructions are provided, the modules are executed in the given sequence. The sequence can be explicitly defined through numbered steps or implicitly followed based on the order in which the modules are written. This elementary flow pattern is commonly used in most processing, including some complex problems.

Selection Logic (Conditional Flow)

Selection Logic involves conditions or parameters that determine which module will be executed among several written modules. Structures that employ this logic are known as Conditional Structures, which can be categorized into three types.

1. Single AlternativeThis structure has the form:

```
If (condition) then:
     [Module A]
[End of If structure]
```

2. Double Alternative, This structure has the form:
```
If (Condition), then:
     [code]
Else:
     [code]
[End if structure]
```

3. Multiple Alternatives, This structure has the form:

```
If (condition A), then:
     [code for A]
Else if (condition B), then:
     [code for B]

        ..

        ..

Else if (condition Z), then:
     [code for Z]
[End If structure]
```

Iteration Logic (Repetitive Flow)

The Iteration logic utilizes a loop that consists of a repeat statement followed by a module called the loop body. There are two types of these structures:

1. Repeat-For Structure

```
Repeat for i = A to B by I:
    [Code]
[End of loop]
```

Here, A represents the initial value, B represents the end value, and I represents the increment. The loop will terminate when i is greater than B. K will either increase or decrease based on whether I is positive or negative respectively.

2. Repeat-While Structure

It also uses a condition to control the loop. This structure has the form:

```
Repeat while [condition]:
    [Codes]
[End of Loop]
```

Hand-on: Control Structures

Selection Logic (if, elif, else)

Exercise 1: Grading System

Write a Python program that takes a student's score as input and then prints out their grade based on the following criteria:

If the score is between 90 and 100 (inclusive), print "A"
If the score is between 80 and 89 (inclusive), print "B"
If the score is between 70 and 79 (inclusive), print "C"
If the score is between 60 and 69 (inclusive), print "D"
If the score is below 60, print "F"

Type the following code in a new python script using VSCode and saved in the folder of your choice as file name such as ex1.py and run the script in the terminal:

```python
# Exercise 1: Grading System
score = int(input("Enter the student's score: "))

if 90 <= score <= 100:
    grade = "A"
elif 80 <= score < 90:
    grade = "B"
elif 70 <= score < 80:
    grade = "C"
elif 60 <= score < 70:
    grade = "D"
else:
    grade = "F"

print(f"The student's grade is: {grade}")
```

| PROBLEMS | OUTPUT | DEBUG CONSOLE | TERMINAL | PORTS |

```
● PS C:\Users\teokk> cd C:\myproject\\day2
● PS C:\myproject\day2> python .\ex1.py
  Enter the student's score: 50
  The student's grade is: F
● PS C:\myproject\day2> python .\ex1.py
  Enter the student's score: 95
  The student's grade is: A
● PS C:\myproject\day2> python .\ex1.py
  Enter the student's score: 65
  The student's grade is: D
○ PS C:\myproject\day2> █
```

Figure 8 terminal output of running ex1.py

Exercise 2: Ticket Pricing

Write a Python program that calculates the ticket price for a theme park based on the age of the visitor:

If the age is 0-2, the ticket is free.
If the age is 3-12, the ticket costs $10.
If the age is 13-65, the ticket costs $20.
If the age is 66 or older, the ticket costs $15.

Type the following code in a new python script using VSCode and saved in the folder of your choice as file name such as ex2.py and run the script in the terminal:

```python
# Exercise 2: Ticket Pricing
age = int(input("Enter the visitor's age: "))

if 0 <= age <= 2:
    ticket_price = 0
elif 3 <= age <= 12:
    ticket_price = 10
elif 13 <= age <= 65:
    ticket_price = 20
else:
    ticket_price = 15

print(f"The ticket price is: ${ticket_price}")
```

```
● PS C:\Users\teokk> cd C:\myproject\day2
● PS C:\myproject\day2> python .\ex2.py
  Enter the visitor's age: 1
  The ticket price is: $0
● PS C:\myproject\day2> python .\ex2.py
  Enter the visitor's age: 60
  The ticket price is: $20
● PS C:\myproject\day2> python .\ex2.py
  Enter the visitor's age: 70
  The ticket price is: $15
○ PS C:\myproject\day2> ▌
```

Figure 9 terminal output of running ex2.py

Exercise 3: Leap Year Checker

Write a Python program that checks if a given year is a leap year. A year is a leap year if it is divisible by 4, except for years that are divisible by 100 but not divisible by 400.

Type the following code in a new python script using VSCode and saved in the folder of your choice as file name such as ex3.py and run the script in the terminal:

```
# Exercise 3: Leap Year Checker
year = int(input("Enter a year: "))

if (year % 4 == 0 and year % 100 != 0) or (year % 400 == 0):
    print(f"{year} is a leap year.")
else:
    print(f"{year} is not a leap year.")
```

```
PS C:\Users\teokk> cd C:\myproject\day2
PS C:\myproject\day2> python .\ex3.py
Enter a year: 1995
1995 is not a leap year.
PS C:\myproject\day2> python .\ex3.py
Enter a year: 2000
2000 is a leap year.
PS C:\myproject\day2> python .\ex3.py
Enter a year: 2023
2023 is not a leap year.
PS C:\myproject\day2>
```

Figure 10 terminal output of running ex3.py

Iteration Logic (while, for)

Exercise 4: iteration Logic (while)Print 1 to 10

Write a Python program that prints numbers from 1 to 10 using a while loop.

Type the following code in a new python script using VSCode and saved in the folder of your choice as file name such as ex4.py and run the script in the terminal:

```
# Solution for ex4:
num = 1
while num <= 10:
    print(num)
    num += 1
```

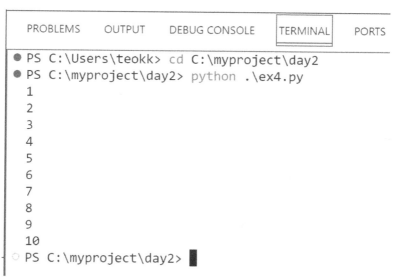

Figure 10 terminal output of running ex4.py

Exercise 5: iteration Logic (for)Print 1 to 10

Write a Python program that prints numbers from 1 to 10 using a while loop.

Type the following code in a new python script using VSCode and saved in the folder of your choice as file name such as ex5.py and run the script in the terminal:

```
# Solution for ex5 (Using a for loop):
for num in range(1, 11):
    print(num)
```

PROBLEMS	OUTPUT	DEBUG CONSOLE	TERMINAL	PORTS

```
● PS C:\Users\teokk> cd C:\myproject\day2
● PS C:\myproject\day2> python .\ex5.py
  1
  2
  3
  4
  5
  6
  7
  8
  9
  10
○ PS C:\myproject\day2> ▌
```

Figure 11 terminal output of running ex5.py

Exercise 6: sum of even numbers

Write a Python program that calculates the sum of all even numbers from 1 to 50 using a while loop.

Type the following code in a new python script using VSCode and saved in the folder of your choice as file name such as ex6.py and run the script in the terminal:

```
# Solution:
num = 2
sum_even = 0

while num <= 50:
    sum_even += num
    num += 2

print("Sum of even numbers from 1 to 50:", sum_even)
```

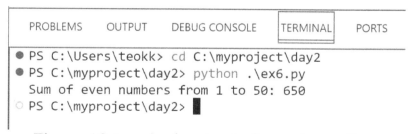

Figure 12 terminal output of running ex6.py

Exercise 7: guess a secret number

Write a Python program that prompts the user to guess a secret number between 1 and 100. Keep prompting the user until they guess the correct number.

Type the following code in a new python script using VSCode and saved in the folder of your choice as file name such as ex7.py and run the script in the terminal:

```python
# Solution:
import random
#get a random number 1 - 100
secret_number = random.randint(1, 100)
guessed = False

while not guessed:
    guess = int(input("Guess the secret number (between 1 and 100): "))
    if guess == secret_number:
        print("Congratulations! You guessed the secret number.")
        guessed = True
    elif guess < secret_number:
        print("Try higher.")
    else:
        print("Try lower.")
```

```
PS C:\Users\teokk> cd C:\myproject\day2
PS C:\myproject\day2> python .\ex7.py
Guess the secret number (between 1 and 100): 5
Try higher.
Guess the secret number (between 1 and 100): 50
Try lower.
Guess the secret number (between 1 and 100): 25
Try higher.
Guess the secret number (between 1 and 100): 35
Try higher.
Guess the secret number (between 1 and 100): 40
Try lower.
Guess the secret number (between 1 and 100): 36
Try higher.
Guess the secret number (between 1 and 100): 37
Congratulations! You guessed the secret number.
PS C:\myproject\day2> 
```

Figure 13 terminal output of running ex7.py

Exercise 8: factorial computation

Write a Python program that calculates the factorial of a given number using a while loop.

Type the following code in a new python script using VSCode and saved in the folder of your choice as file name such as ex8.py and run the script in the terminal:

```python
# Solution:
def factorial(n):
    result = 1
    while n > 0:
        result *= n
        n -= 1
    return result

num = int(input("Enter a number: "))
if num < 0:
    print("Factorial is not defined for negative numbers.")
else:
    print(f"The factorial of {num} is {factorial(num)}")
```

PROBLEMS	OUTPUT	DEBUG CONSOLE	TERMINAL	PORTS

```
● PS C:\Users\teokk> cd C:\myproject\day2
● PS C:\myproject\day2> python .\ex8.py
  Enter a number: 10
  The factorial of 10 is 3628800
○ PS C:\myproject\day2>
```

Figure 14 terminal output of running ex8.py

Control flow and Indention

Control flow and indentation are fundamental concepts in Python programming. They determine the order in which statements are executed in your code and how the code is structured. Python uses indentation to define blocks of code, which is different from many other programming languages that use braces or other symbols for this purpose.

Control flow refers to the order in which statements in your code are executed. Python provides several control flow structures to make your code more flexible and powerful:

Indentation is a crucial part of Python's syntax. Unlike many other programming languages that use braces or keywords to define blocks of code, Python uses whitespace indentation. Indentation defines the scope of code blocks and helps to maintain readability.

Here's an example of indentation in Python:

```
if condition:
    # This code is indented and part of the if block
    print("Condition is True")
else:
    # This code is indented and part of the else block
    print("Condition is False")
# This code is not indented and is outside the if-else block
print("This is always executed")
```

It's essential to maintain consistent indentation throughout your code. Typically, Python developers use four spaces for each level of indentation. Most code editors and IDEs automatically handle the indentation for you.

In summary, control flow and indentation are essential concepts in Python programming. Control flow structures like conditional statements and loops allow you to control the flow of your program, while proper indentation ensures that your code is well-structured and readable.

Day 3: Functions and Modules

Day 3: Functions and Modules

Functions Definition

Functions are essential in Python programming as they are blocks of reusable code that execute specific tasks when called. By organizing and structuring code, functions enhance modularity and facilitate code reusability. Here is an overview of functions in Python:

Defining a Function:

In Python, you define a function using the "def" keyword, followed by the function name, a pair of parentheses, and a colon. The function name should be descriptive and adhere to naming conventions (lowercase letters with underscores for readability). Parameters can also be specified within the parentheses if the function requires input.

Example of a function definition of the function name *greet* and calling the function *greet*.

```
def greet(name):
    """This function greets the person passed in as a parameter."""
    print(f"Hello, {name}!")

# Calling the function
greet("Alice")
```

The code snippet you provided defines a Python function named greet with one parameter, name, which has a default value of "Guest" if no value is provided when calling the function. Let's break down how this function works and how it is called:

```
greet()
```

When called without any argument, the name parameter defaults to "Guest". So, this call prints "Hello, Guest!" to the console.

When called with an argument, such as "Alice", the name parameter takes the provided value. In this case, the function prints "Hello, Alice!" to the console.

```
greet("Alice")
```

Function Parameters:

Functions can accept zero or more parameters (also called arguments). Parameters are values that are passed into the function when it's called and can be used within the function. Parameters can have default values if not provided when calling the function.

Function Return Values:

A function can return a value using the return statement. This value can be used elsewhere in your program. If there is no return statement, the function returns None by default.

```
def add(x, y):
    return x + y

result = add(3, 5)
print(result)  # Outputs 8
```

Scope:

Variables defined inside a function have local scope, which means they are only accessible within that function. Variables defined outside of any function have global scope and can be accessed from anywhere in the code.

x = 10 # Global variable

def func():
    y = 5 # Local variable
    print(x) # Accessing the global variable
    print(y) # Accessing the local variable

func()
print(x)   # Accessing the global variable outside the function is fine
print(y)   # This would result in an error because y is not defined globally

You can type the provided code in VSCODE and run it in the terminal to observe the output and gain a better understanding.

Introduction to Python Modules

In Python, a module is a file containing Python code that can be reused in other Python programs. Modules allow you to organize your code into separate files, making it more maintainable and promoting code reusability. They are an essential concept in Python programming, enabling you to create libraries of functions, variables, and classes for various purposes.

Creating Modules:

To create a module, you typically save a Python script with a .py extension. For example, you can create a module named my_module.py to encapsulate related functionality.
Importing Modules:

To use a module in your Python program, you need to import it using the import statement.

import my_module

You can also import specific attributes (functions, variables, or classes) from a module using the from ... import syntax.

from my_module import my_function

To import all attributes from a module into the current namespace, you can use the * wildcard.

from my_*module* import *

Module Search Paths:

Python looks for modules in specific directories defined by the sys.path list. These directories include the current working directory and the standard library directories. You can add custom directories to sys.path if your modules are not in the standard locations.
Module Namespaces:

When you import a module, it creates a new namespace containing all the attributes defined in that module. This avoids naming conflicts with other parts of your code.
Using Module Attributes:

You can access attributes from a module using dot notation. For example, if my_module contains a function named my_function, you can call it like this:

my_module.my_function()

Standard Library Modules:

Python comes with a rich standard library that includes modules for various purposes, such as file I/O, data manipulation, networking, and more. You can use these modules to perform common tasks without reinventing the wheel.

Creating Your Own Modules:

Creating custom modules allows you to organize your code logically and make it more modular. You can package related functions, variables, or classes into separate modules and import them as needed in different parts of your program.

Best Practices:

When working with modules, it's good practice to provide clear and concise documentation, known as docstrings, for functions and classes within your module. This helps other developers understand how to use your code effectively.

Module Aliases:

You can give imported modules or attributes aliases to simplify usage or avoid naming conflicts.

```
import my_module as mm
mm.my_function()
```

Python modules are a powerful way to organize and reuse code, whether you're working on small scripts or large-scale applications. They promote code modularity, readability, and maintainability, making it easier to collaborate with others and build complex software systems.

Hand-on: Function

Exercise 1: Calculator Function

Create a function that performs basic mathematical operations (addition, subtraction, multiplication, and division) on two numbers.

Type the following code in a new python script using VSCode and saved in the folder of your choice as file name such as ex1.py and run the script in the terminal:

```python
def calculator(num1, num2, operator):
    if operator == '+':
        return num1 + num2
    elif operator == '-':
        return num1 - num2
    elif operator == '*':
        return num1 * num2
    elif operator == '/':
        if num2 == 0:
            return "Division by zero is not allowed."
        return num1 / num2
    else:
        return "Invalid operator"

# Example usage:
result = calculator(5, 3, '+')
print(result)  # Output: 8
```

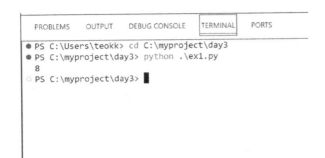

Figure 15 terminal output of running ex1.py

Exercise 2: Palindrome Checker

Write a function to check if a given word is a palindrome (reads the same forwards and backwards).

Type the following code in a new python script using VSCode and saved in the folder of your choice as file name such as ex2.py and run the script in the terminal:

```
def is_palindrome(word):
    return word == word[::-1]

# Example usage:
print(is_palindrome("racecar")) # Output: True
print(is_palindrome("hello"))   # Output: False
```

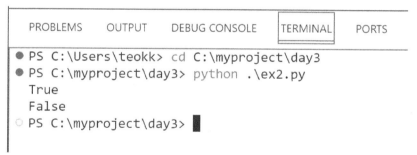

```
PROBLEMS    OUTPUT    DEBUG CONSOLE    TERMINAL    PORTS

● PS C:\Users\teokk> cd C:\myproject\day3
● PS C:\myproject\day3> python .\ex2.py
  True
  False
○ PS C:\myproject\day3> █
```

Figure 16 terminal output of running ex2.py

Exercise 3: Factorial Function

Implement a function to calculate the factorial of a positive integer.

Type the following code in a new python script using VSCode and saved in the folder of your choice as file name such as ex3.py and run the script in the terminal:

```python
def factorial(n):
    if n == 0:
        return 1
    else:
        return n * factorial(n - 1)

# Example usage:
result = factorial(5)
print(result)  # Output: 120
```

PROBLEMS	OUTPUT	DEBUG CONSOLE	TERMINAL	PORTS

```
● PS C:\Users\teokk> cd C:\myproject\day3
● PS C:\myproject\day3> python .\ex3.py
  120
○ PS C:\myproject\day3> █
```

Figure 17 terminal output of running ex3.py

Day 4: Working with Data

Day 4: Working with Data

Reading Assignment: Introduction to data structures

Data structures are fundamental components in programming that allow you to store, organize, and manipulate data efficiently. In Python, three commonly used data structures are lists, tuples, and dictionaries. Each of these structures has its own characteristics and use cases.

Lists

Lists are ordered collections of items that can store elements of different data types.

They are defined using square brackets [ ] and can contain zero or more elements.

Lists are mutable, which means you can change their contents (add, remove, or modify elements).

Example:

my_list = [1, 2, 3, "hello", 5.0]

Tuples

Tuples are similar to lists but are immutable, meaning their contents cannot be changed once defined.

They are defined using parentheses ( ) and can also contain elements of different data types.

Tuples are often used for data that should not be modified, such as coordinates or configurations.

Example:

my_tuple = (1, 2, 3, "hello", 5.0)

Dictionaries

Dictionaries are collections of key-value pairs, where each key is associated with a value.

They are defined using curly braces { } or the dict() constructor.

Dictionaries are unordered, meaning the order of elements is not guaranteed (introduced in Python 3.7+).

Example:

my_dict = {"name": "John", "age": 30, "city": "New York"}

Accessing elements

Lists and tuples: Elements are accessed using indexing (e.g., my_list[0], my_tuple[2]).
Dictionaries: Values are accessed using keys (e.g., my_dict["name"]).

Adding elements

Lists: Use the append() method to add an element at the end of the list.
Tuples: Since tuples are immutable, you cannot add elements after creation.
Dictionaries: Assign a new key-value pair to add an element.

Modifying elements

Lists: Use indexing to modify elements (e.g., my_list[0] = 42).
Tuples: Since tuples are immutable, you cannot modify elements after creation.

Dictionaries: Change the value associated with a key.
Removing elements:

Lists: Use methods like remove(), pop(), or del to remove elements.
Tuples: Since tuples are immutable, you cannot remove elements after creation.
Dictionaries: Use the pop() method to remove key-value pairs.
These data structures are essential tools for organizing and processing data in Python. Choosing the right one for your specific task is crucial for efficient and readable code. Lists are versatile for storing collections of items, tuples are suitable for immutable data, and dictionaries excel at key-value pair mappings.

Indexing:

Indexing refers to accessing individual elements within a data structure. In Python, indexing is zero-based, which means the first element has an index of 0, the second element has an index of 1, and so on.

Here's how indexing works with different data structures:

Lists:

```
my_list = [10, 20, 30, 40, 50]
first_element = my_list[0]  # Access the first element (10)
third_element = my_list[2]  # Access the third element (30)
```

Strings:

```
my_string = "Hello, World!"
first_char = my_string[0]   # Access the first character ('H')
sixth_char = my_string[5]   # Access the sixth character (',')
```

Slicing:

Slicing allows you to extract a portion of a data structure, creating a new one with the selected elements. The basic syntax for slicing is start:stop:step, where start is the index where the slice begins, stop is the index where it ends (exclusive), and step is the increment between elements.

Here's how slicing works:

Lists:

```
my_list = [10, 20, 30, 40, 50]
sublist = my_list[1:4]     # Extract elements at index 1, 2, and 3 ([20, 30, 40])
even_indices = my_list[::2] # Extract elements at even indices ([10, 30, 50])
```

Strings:

```
my_string = "Hello, World!"
substring = my_string[7:12]   # Extract characters from index 7 to 11 ('World')
every_other_char = my_string[::2]  # Extract every other character ('Hlo ol!')
```

Keep in mind that the stop index in slicing is exclusive, so the element at the stop index itself won't be included in the result. If you omit start and stop, the slice will include all elements. If you omit step, it defaults to 1.

Hand-on: Working with data

Exercise 1: Indexing Lists

Access specific elements within a list using indexing. Retrieve the second element and the last element from a list of fruits.

Type the following code in a new python script using VSCode and saved in the folder of your choice as file name such as ex1.py and run the script in the terminal:

```python
fruits = ["apple", "banana", "cherry", "date", "elderberry"]
second_fruit = fruits[1]  # "banana"
last_fruit = fruits[-1]   # "elderberry"
print("Second fruit:", second_fruit)
print("Last fruit:", last_fruit)
```

PROBLEMS	OUTPUT	DEBUG CONSOLE	TERMINAL	PORTS

```
● PS C:\Users\teokk> cd C:\myproject\day4
● PS C:\myproject\day4> python .\ex1.py
  Second fruit: banana
  Last fruit: elderberry
○ PS C:\myproject\day4> ▮
```

Figure 18 terminal output of running ex1.py

Exercise 2: Slicing Lists

Create new lists by extracting specific subsets of elements from an existing list. Extract a subset containing "banana," "cherry," and "date," as well as a subset with every other fruit.

Type the following code in a new python script using VSCode and saved in the folder of your choice as file name such as ex2.py and run the script in the terminal:

```
fruits = ["apple", "banana", "cherry", "date", "elderberry"]
selected_fruits = fruits[1:4]  # ["banana", "cherry", "date"]
every_other_fruit = fruits[::2]  # ["apple", "cherry", "elderberry"]

print("Selected fruits:", selected_fruits)
print("Every other fruit:", every_other_fruit)
```

PROBLEMS	OUTPUT	DEBUG CONSOLE	TERMINAL	PORTS

```
● PS C:\Users\teokk> cd C:\myproject\day4
● PS C:\myproject\day4> python .\ex2.py
  Selected fruits: ['banana', 'cherry', 'date']
  Every other fruit: ['apple', 'cherry', 'elderberry']
○ PS C:\myproject\day4> █
```

Figure 19 terminal output of running ex2.py

Exercise 3: Indexing Strings

Access individual characters within a string using indexing. Retrieve the first and sixth characters from a given sentence.

Type the following code in a new python script using VSCode and saved in the folder of your choice as file name such as ex3.py and run the script in the terminal:

```python
sentence = "This is a sample sentence."
first_char = sentence[0]  # "T"
sixth_char = sentence[5]  # "i"

print("First character:", first_char)
print("Sixth character:", sixth_char)
```

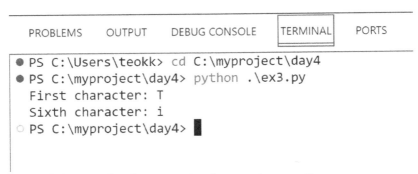

Figure 20 terminal output of running ex3.py

Exercise 4: Slicing Strings

Create new strings by extracting substrings from an existing string. Extract the word "sample" and a string with every other character from a given sentence.

Type the following code in a new python script using VSCode and saved in the folder of your choice as file name such as ex4.py and run the script in the terminal:

```
sentence = "This is a sample sentence."
substring = sentence[10:16]   # "sample"
even_chars = sentence[::2]    # "Ti ssasme etne"

print("Substring:", substring)
print("Every other character:", even_chars)
```

PROBLEMS	OUTPUT	DEBUG CONSOLE	TERMINAL	PORTS

```
● PS C:\Users\teokk> cd C:\myproject\day4
● PS C:\myproject\day4> python .\ex4.py
  Substring: sample
  Every other character: Ti sasml etne
○ PS C:\myproject\day4> ▊
```

Figure 21 terminal output of running ex4.py

Day 5: Data Analysis with Pandas

Day 5: Data Analysis with Pandas

Reading Assignment: Introduction to Pandas dataframes

Pandas is a popular data manipulation library in Python that provides powerful tools for working with structured data. One of its core data structures is the DataFrame, which is similar to a table in a relational database or a spreadsheet in Excel. DataFrames are incredibly versatile and are widely used for data analysis, data cleaning, and data preparation tasks. In this introduction, we'll explore the key concepts and capabilities of Pandas DataFrames.

What is a DataFrame?

A DataFrame is a two-dimensional, size-mutable, and heterogeneous tabular data structure with labeled axes (rows and columns). This means that you can think of it as a table with rows and columns, where each column can hold different data types (e.g., integers, strings, floats, etc.). The rows and columns are labeled, allowing for easy referencing and manipulation of data.

Creating a DataFrame

You can create a DataFrame from various data sources, including:

Lists or Numpy arrays: You can construct a DataFrame by passing a list of lists or a 2D NumPy array to the Pandas DataFrame constructor.

```
import pandas as pd

data = [['Alice', 25], ['Bob', 30], ['Charlie', 35]]
df = datagram(data, columns=['Name', 'Age'])
```

You can also create a DataFrame from a dictionary where keys represent column names and values are lists or arrays of data.

```
import pandas as pd

data = [['Alice', 25], ['Bob', 30], ['Charlie', 35]]
df = pd.DataFrame(data, columns=['Name', 'Age'])
```

Loading from external data sources: Pandas supports reading data from various file formats like CSV, Excel, SQL databases, and more.

```
# Reading a CSV file into a DataFrame
df = pd.read_csv('data.csv')
```

DataFrame Operations

Once you have a DataFrame, you can perform a wide range of operations on it:

Viewing Data: You can quickly inspect the contents of a DataFrame using functions like head(), tail(), or sample() to see the first few, last few, or random rows of data.

Selecting Data: You can select specific rows and columns using labels or numerical indices. For example, df['ColumnName'] selects a specific column, and df.loc[row_index] selects a specific row.

Filtering Data: You can filter rows based on conditions using boolean indexing. For instance, df[df['Age'] > 30] selects rows where the 'Age' column is greater than 30.

Data Manipulation: You can perform various operations on the data, such as adding new columns, renaming columns, and applying mathematical operations.

Aggregation and Grouping: Pandas allows you to group data and compute aggregate statistics using functions like groupby() and agg().

Merging and Joining: You can combine multiple DataFrames using operations like concatenation, merging, and joining to analyze data from different sources.

Pandas DataFrames are an essential tool for data manipulation and analysis in Python. They provide a flexible and efficient way to work with structured data, making it easier to explore, clean, and analyze data for various data science and analytical tasks. In this introduction, we've covered the basics, but there is much more to explore as you dive deeper into Pandas and its capabilities.

Hand-on Panda DataFrame

Exercise 1 Generate sales_data.csv

For the purpose of next few lab, we will generate a CSV file with sample sales data using Python. You can then save it as "sales_data.csv." Here's a Python script to generate sample sales data and save it as a CSV file:

Type the following code in a new python script using VSCode and saved in the folder of your choice as file name such as ex1.py and run the script in the terminal:

```python
import pandas as pd
import random
from faker import Faker
import csv

# Initialize Faker for generating random product names
fake = Faker()

# Generate sample data
data = []
for _ in range(100): # Generating data for 100 sales records, you can adjust this number
    date = fake.date_between(start_date='-1y', end_date='today')  # Random date within the last year
    product = fake.word() # Random product name
    units_sold = random.randint(1, 100)  # Random units sold between 1 and 100
```

```python
    revenue = round(random.uniform(10, 2000), 2)  # Random revenue
between $10 and $2000
    data.append([date, product, units_sold, revenue])

# Create a Pandas DataFrame
df = pd.DataFrame(data, columns=['Date', 'Product', 'Units Sold',
'Revenue'])

# Save the DataFrame as a CSV file
df.to_csv('sales_data.csv',index=False,
quoting=csv.QUOTE_NONNUMERIC)

print("CSV file 'sale_data.csv' has been generated.")
```

This script uses the Faker library to generate random product names, and it creates 100 rows of sample sales data with random dates, product names, units sold, and revenue values. The data is then saved to a CSV file named "sales_data.csv" in the same directory as your Python script. You can adjust the number of records generated by changing the loop limit.

Make sure you have the Faker library installed before running ex1.py. You can install it using pip:

pip install faker

This script and subsequent exercises used pandas library. Make sure you have the FPanda library installed before running ex1.py. You can install it using pip:

pip install pandas

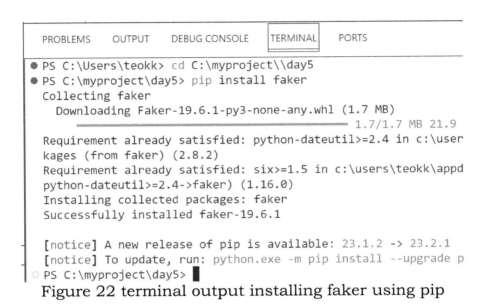

Figure 22 terminal output installing faker using pip

Once you are done installing faker, you cam run ex1.py as in previous exercises.

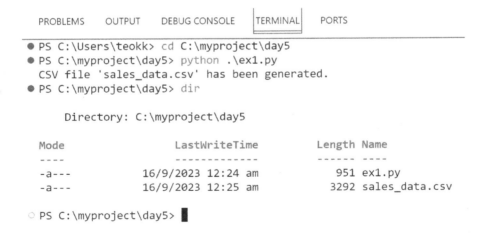

Figure 23 terminal output of ex1.py using pip

You can check your folder to confirm that sales_data.csv was generated. You could open the file using notepad or excel to view the content.

Date	Product	Units Sold	Revenue
3/5/2023	against	23	81.14
27/12/2022	evidence	61	198.26
29/8/2023	not	64	169.83
30/4/2023	goal	44	803.88
4/5/2023	east	69	1129.77
20/2/2023	focus	9	1035.4
10/6/2023	Democrat	58	1451.4
1/12/2022	green	27	333.48

Figure 24 screenshot portion of sale_data.csv generated

Exerecise 2: load data

To perform hands-on exercises for selecting and filtering data using pandas with a CSV file named "sale_data.csv," you'll first need to read the CSV file into a pandas DataFrame. I'll assume you have the "sale_data.csv" file generated in exercise 1 in the same directory as your Python script.

Type the following code in a new python script using VSCode and saved in the folder of your choice as file name such as ex2.py and run the script in the terminal:

```
import pandas as pd

# Read the CSV file into a DataFrame
df = pd.read_csv('sale_data.csv')

# Display the first few rows of the DataFrame to understand its
structure
print(df.head())
```

Note that the output of your script might look abit different from mine in the figure below as the sale_data.csv you generated and mine would have different content as it was generated randomly.

```
● PS C:\Users\teokk> cd C:\myproject\\day5
● PS C:\myproject\day5> python .\ex2.py
          Date   Product   Units Sold   Revenue
0   2022-09-23       bag           34   1764.53
1   2022-09-27     level           95    827.15
2   2022-11-23   produce           67    779.53
3   2023-04-03     short           89   1868.39
4   2023-09-14     mouth           28    730.07
○ PS C:\myproject\day5> █
```

Figure 25 terminal output of running ex2.py

Exerecise 3: selecting specific columns

Now that you have leant how to load the data, let's proceed to select the 'Date' and 'Revenue' columns

Type the following code in a new python script using VSCode and saved in the folder of your choice as file name such as ex3.py and run the script in the terminal:

import pandas as pd

 # Read the CSV file into a DataFrame
df = pd.read_csv('sale_data.csv')
selected_columns = df[['Date', 'Revenue']]
print("\nSelected Columns:")
print(selected_columns)

	PROBLEMS	OUTPUT	DEBUG CONSOLE	TERMINAL	PORTS

```
            Date   Revenue
0     2022-09-23  1764.53
1     2022-09-27   827.15
2     2022-11-23   779.53
3     2023-04-03  1868.39
4     2023-09-14   730.07
..          ...      ...
95    2023-06-13  1913.37
96    2023-09-11  1478.73
97    2023-07-07   172.33
98    2022-11-06   807.83
99    2022 02 27   215 35
```

Figure 26 terminal output of running ex3.py

Exercise 4: Filtering Rows Based on a Condition

Filter rows where the 'Units Sold' is greater than 80:

Type the following code in a new python script using VSCode and saved in the folder of your choice as file name such as ex3.py and run the script in the terminal:

```python
import pandas as pd

# Read the CSV file into a DataFrame
df = pd.read_csv('sale_data.csv')
high_units_sold = df[df['Units Sold'] > 80]
print("\nRows with Units Sold >80:")
print(high_units_sold)
```

```
● PS C:\Users\teokk> cd C:\myproject\day5
● PS C:\myproject\day5> python .\ex4.py

Rows with Units Sold >80:
            Date      Product  Units Sold   Revenue
1     2022-09-27        level          95    827.15
3     2023-04-03        short          89   1868.39
6     2023-03-22        paper          83   1558.26
15    2023-07-18       manage          86    846.50
16    2022-11-23       happen          88    463.52
18    2023-01-11       beyond          93   1411.69
19    2022-10-12       option          89   1657.56
21    2023-09-12      picture          96    996.72
36    2022-11-21       street          87    755.35
41    2022-10-09         take          83   1863.77
50    2023-08-25       leader          97   1014.34
56    2023-07-13        never          81    108.33
63    2023-04-14         what          95    602.88
69    2023-05-07        short          84    694.06
73    2023-05-26    treatment          85   1284.82
74    2023-06-07       matter          83   1691.84
76    2023-02-17          ago          88    235.41
77    2023-08-05    newspaper          93   1073.15
78    2023-03-05         task          86    226.55
81    2023-04-30         give          82     34.69
83    2023-07-11        image          86   1499.84
91    2022-12-11     increase          82    967.50
95    2023-06-13       rather          97   1913.37
99    2023-02-27      partner          87    215.35
○ PS C:\myproject\day5> █
```

Figure 27 terminal output of running ex4.py

Exerecise 5: Analyzing Sales Data

You have been generated a CSV file named "sales_data.csv" containing sales data for a retail store. Your task is to load this data into a Pandas DataFrame and perform some basic data analysis tasks. The dataset contains the following columns:

- `Date`: The date of the sale.
- `Product`: The name of the product sold.
- `Units Sold`: The number of units sold.
- `Revenue`: The revenue generated from the sale.

Your Tasks:

1. Load the data from "sales_data.csv" into a Pandas DataFrame.
2. Display the first 5 rows of the DataFrame to get an overview of the data.
3. Calculate the total revenue for the entire dataset.
4. Find the product that generated the highest revenue.
5. Calculate the average number of units sold per sale.

Type the following code in a new python script using VSCode and saved in the folder of your choice as file name such as ex5.py and run the script in the terminal:

```python
# Import Pandas library
import pandas as pd

# Load the data into a DataFrame
df = pd.read_csv('sales_data.csv')

# Display the first 5 rows
print(df.head())

# Calculate total revenue
total_revenue = df['Revenue'].sum()
print("Total Revenue:", total_revenue)

# Find the product with the highest revenue
highest_revenue_product = df[df['Revenue'] ==
df['Revenue'].max()]['Product'].values[0]
print("Product with Highest Revenue:", highest_revenue_product)

# Calculate average units sold per sale
average_units_sold = df['Units Sold'].mean()
print("Average Units Sold per Sale:", average_units_sold)
```

```
PROBLEMS    OUTPUT    DEBUG CONSOLE    TERMINAL    PORTS

● PS C:\Users\teokk> cd C:\myproject\day5
● PS C:\myproject\day5> python .\ex2.py
            Date    Product   Units Sold   Revenue
  0   2023-05-03   against          23       81.14
  1   2022-12-27   evidence         61      198.26
  2   2023-08-29        not          64      169.83
  3   2023-04-30       goal          44      803.88
  4   2023-05-04       east          69     1129.77
  Total Revenue: 90747.40999999999
  Product with Highest Revenue: four
  Average Units Sold per Sale: 53.15
○ PS C:\myproject\day5> █
```

Figure 28 terminal output of ex5.py using pip

In this exercise, we first load the sales data from a CSV file into a Pandas DataFrame. Then, we display the first 5 rows of the DataFrame to understand the data structure. Then we learnt to select by columns and filter row by condition. Next, we put everything together to perform sale analysis in exercise 5. In exercise 5, we calculate the total revenue by summing the "Revenue" column. We find the product with the highest revenue by filtering the DataFrame based on the maximum revenue value. Finally, we calculate the average units sold per sale using the mean() function.

These exercises demonstrates some basic data analysis tasks you can perform with Pandas DataFrames, such as data loading, exploration, aggregation, and filtering. You can further expand on these tasks and explore more advanced analysis techniques as you become more familiar with Pandas.

Day 6: Data Visualization with Matplotlib

Day 6: Data Visualization with Matplotlib

Reading Assignment: Introduction to data visualization

Data visualization is a powerful tool that allows us to transform raw data into meaningful and actionable insights through graphical representations. In an era defined by the deluge of information, data visualization plays a crucial role in helping individuals and organizations make informed decisions, identify patterns, and communicate complex ideas effectively.

At its core, data visualization is the art and science of presenting data in a visual format, such as charts, graphs, maps, and interactive dashboards. These visual representations bring data to life, making it more accessible and understandable to a wide audience, regardless of their level of expertise in the subject matter. By translating numbers and statistics into visual cues, data visualization helps us recognize trends, outliers, and relationships that might otherwise go unnoticed in tables of raw data.

The importance of data visualization extends across various domains, including business, science, healthcare, education, journalism, and government. In the business world, it aids in market analysis, performance tracking, and strategic planning. In scientific research, it facilitates the interpretation of experimental results and the communication of findings. In healthcare, it supports clinical decision-making and patient outcomes analysis. In education, it enhances the comprehension of complex concepts, and in journalism, it enables compelling storytelling with data.

This introduction to data visualization will explore its fundamental concepts, the tools and techniques used to create visualizations, the different types of visualizations, and the best practices for designing effective and informative visuals. Whether you are a data analyst, a business executive, a researcher, or simply someone interested in making sense of data, understanding the principles of data visualization will empower you to unlock the hidden insights within your data and communicate them clearly to others.

Introduction to Matplotlib

Matplotlib is a widely used Python library that provides a comprehensive framework for creating static, animated, and interactive visualizations. Developed by John D. Hunter in 2003, Matplotlib has since become the go-to library for data visualization and publication-quality graphics in the Python ecosystem. Its flexibility, versatility, and extensive community support make it an invaluable tool for anyone working with data analysis, scientific computing, or any field requiring the visual representation of information.

Matplotlib's strength lies in its ability to produce a wide range of high-quality 2D and, to some extent, 3D visualizations with relatively simple code. Whether you need to create basic line plots, bar charts, scatter plots, histograms, or more complex figures like heatmaps, contour plots, or even animated charts, Matplotlib can meet your needs.

Key features and benefits of Matplotlib include:

1. Easy Integration: Matplotlib seamlessly integrates with various Python libraries and environments, such as NumPy, Pandas, Jupyter notebooks, and other data analysis tools, making it a natural choice for data scientists and engineers.

2. Customization: You have fine-grained control over every aspect of your plots. You can customize colors, line styles, fonts, labels, legends, and many other parameters to match your specific requirements.

3. Publication-Quality Output: Matplotlib is designed to generate high-resolution, publication-quality graphics for scientific papers, reports, presentations, and websites. This makes it a favorite among researchers and academics.

4. Wide Range of Plot Types: It supports various plot types, including line plots, scatter plots, bar charts, pie charts, histograms, error bars, box plots, and more. You can even create complex layouts with multiple subplots.

5. Interactive Features: Matplotlib can be integrated with interactive backends like Jupyter widgets, allowing users to interactively explore and manipulate data in real-time.

6. Extensibility: If the built-in functionality is not enough, Matplotlib is highly extensible. You can create custom plots, add widgets, and even use third-party plugins and styles.

7. Cross-Platform Compatibility: Matplotlib is available on multiple platforms, including Windows, macOS, and Linux, making it accessible to a broad audience.

In this introduction to Matplotlib, we'll explore its basic usage, essential components, and provide examples of common plots. Whether you're a beginner looking to create your first plot or an experienced data scientist wanting to craft intricate visualizations, Matplotlib is a versatile tool that can help you effectively convey your data-driven insights.

Hand-on: Visualization using Matplotlib

Exercise 1: Installation of Matplotlib

To install Matplotlib, simply run the following command:

pip install matplotlib

To verify that Matplotlib has been installed successfully, you can create a simple Python script to import Matplotlib and create a basic plot. Here's an example:

import matplotlib.pyplot as plt

 # Sample data
x = [1, 2, 3, 4, 5]
y = [10, 16, 24, 32, 40]

 # Create a simple line plot
plt.plot(x, y)

 # Show the plot
plt.show()

Save this script as, for exampleex1py, and then run it in VSCODE terminal.

f Matplotlib is correctly installed, a window should appear displaying the plot.

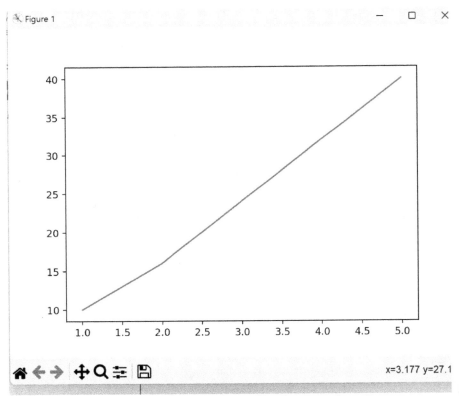

Figure 29 Screenshot of a window displaying the plot.

Exercise 2: Simple Line Plot

Create a basic line plot that shows the population growth of a fictional city over five years. Use the following data:

years = [2018, 2019, 2020, 2021, 2022]
population = [50000, 52000, 55000, 60000, 65000]

Type the following code in a new python script using VSCode and saved in the folder of your choice as file name such as ex2.py and run the script in the terminal:

```
import matplotlib.pyplot as plt

years = [2018, 2019, 2020, 2021, 2022]
population = [50000, 52000, 55000, 60000, 65000]

plt.plot(years, population, marker='o', linestyle='-')
plt.title('Population Growth Over Time')
plt.xlabel('Year')
plt.ylabel('Population')
plt.grid(True)
plt.show()
```

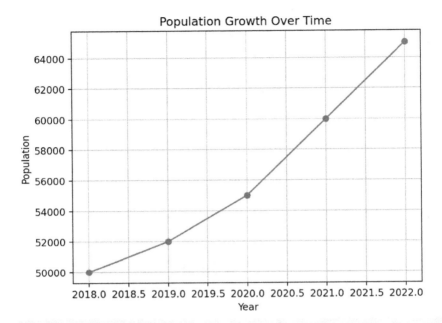

Figure 30 Screenshot of a window displaying the plot.

Exercise 3: Scatter Plot with Color Mapping

Create a scatter plot that shows the relationship between the number of hours studied and test scores for a group of students. Use the following data:

hours_studied = [2, 3, 5, 1, 4, 6, 2, 5, 7, 8]
test_scores = [65, 70, 80, 55, 75, 90, 60, 85, 95, 100]

Type the following code in a new python script using VSCode and saved in the folder of your choice as file name such as ex3.py and run the script in the terminal:

```
import matplotlib.pyplot as plt
import numpy as np

hours_studied = [2, 3, 5, 1, 4, 6, 2, 5, 7, 8]
test_scores = [65, 70, 80, 55, 75, 90, 60, 85, 95, 100]

# Map color to test scores
colors = np.array(test_scores)

plt.scatter(hours_studied, test_scores, c=colors, cmap='viridis')
plt.title('Relationship between Hours Studied and Test Scores')
plt.xlabel('Hours Studied')
plt.ylabel('Test Scores')
plt.colorbar(label='Test Scores')
plt.grid(True)
plt.show()
```

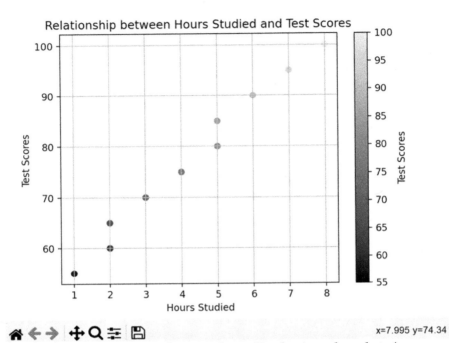

Figure 31 Screenshot of a window displaying the plot. (your plot should be in color)

Exercise 4: Bar Chart

Create a bar chart that displays the monthly sales revenue for a store in the year 2021.

Type the following code in a new python script using VSCode and saved in the folder of your choice as file name such as ex4.py and run the script in the terminal:

```python
import matplotlib.pyplot as plt

months = ['Jan', 'Feb', 'Mar', 'Apr', 'May', 'Jun', 'Jul', 'Aug', 'Sep', 'Oct', 'Nov', 'Dec']
sales_revenue = [15000, 18000, 20000, 22000, 25000, 28000, 30000, 31000, 29000, 27000, 24000, 22000]

plt.bar(months, sales_revenue)
plt.title('Monthly Sales Revenue in 2021')
plt.xlabel('Month')
plt.ylabel('Sales Revenue ($)')
plt.xticks(rotation=45)
plt.grid(axis='y')
plt.show()
```

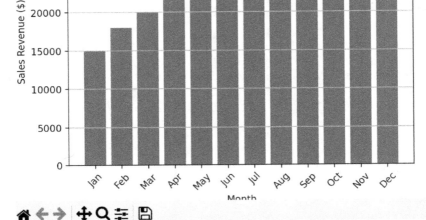

Figure 32 Screenshot of a window displaying the plot. (your plot should be in color)

These exercises cover some fundamental aspects of Matplotlib, including line plots, scatter plots with color mapping, and bar charts. Feel free to modify and extend these exercises to further enhance your Matplotlib skills.

Day 7: Statistics for Data Science

Day 7: Statistics for Data Science

Reading Assignment: Descriptive statistics

Descriptive statistics provide a summary of a dataset, helping us understand its central tendencies and distribution. Here are the definitions of mean, median, and mode:

1. Mean: The mean, often referred to as the average, is calculated by summing up all the values in a dataset and dividing by the total number of values. It provides a measure of the dataset's central tendency. Mathematically, it is represented as:

Mean = Sum of all values / Number of values

2. Median: The median is the middle value of a dataset when all values are arranged in ascending or descending order. If there is an even number of values, the median is the average of the two middle values. The median is less affected by extreme outliers than the mean and is a robust measure of central tendency.

3. Mode:*The mode is the value that appears most frequently in a dataset. A dataset can have one mode (unimodal) or more than one mode (multimodal). In some cases, a dataset may have no mode if all values occur with the same frequency.

Let's illustrate these statistics with an example:

Suppose you have the following dataset representing the number of hours a group of students studied for a test:

{2, 3, 4, 4, 5, 6, 6, 7, 7, 7, 8, 9, 9, 10, 10}

- The mean is calculated by summing all the values and dividing by the total number of values:
  Mean = (2+3+4+4+5+6+6+7+7+7+8+9+9+10+10)/15 =5.92

- The median is the middle value when the data is ordered:
Median = 7

- The mode is the most frequent value, which in this case is 7 since it appears three times, more frequently than any other value in the dataset.

So, for this dataset, the mean is 6.6, the median is 7, and the mode is also 7.

Reading Assignment: Measures of variability

Measures of variability provide insights into how data points in a dataset are spread out or dispersed from the central tendency (mean, median, mode). Two common measures of variability are variance and standard deviation:

1.Variance:** Variance is a statistical measure that quantifies the extent to which data points deviate from the mean. It is calculated by taking the average of the squared differences between each data point and the mean. Mathematically, variance is represented as:

$$\text{Variance}(\sigma^2) = \frac{\sum_{i=1}^{n}(x_i - \mu)^2}{n}$$

-x_i represents each data point.
- mu(μ) is the mean of the dataset.
- n is the total number of data points.

3. Standard Deviation: The standard deviation is a measure of variability that is closely related to variance. It is calculated as the square root of the variance and provides a measure of how spread out the data points are. Mathematically, standard deviation is represented as:

Standard deviation=sqrt(variance)

Standard deviation is often preferred over variance because it is in the same units as the original data, making it more interpretable.

Let's use an example to calculate these measures of variability for a dataset representing the ages of a group of individuals:

{25, 28, 30, 32, 35, 38, 40, 45, 50, 5}

First, calculate the mean:

Mean= (25+28+30+32+35+38+40+45+50+5)/10
=328/10 = 32.8

Next, calculate the variance:
Variance= 154.84

After calculating this, you'll find the variance. Finally, calculate the standard deviation by taking the square root of the variance:

Standard Deviation=sqrt(Variance)= 12.44

These measures will help you understand how the ages in the dataset are dispersed around the mean age of 38.8 years.

Reading Assignment :Probability distributions (normal, binomial)

A simple introduction of the normal and binomial distributions without the mathematical formulas:

Normal Distribution (Gaussian Distribution)

- The normal distribution is often referred to as the bell curve because of its characteristic shape, which resembles a bell.
- In a normal distribution, data tends to cluster around the mean (average) value, and the distribution is symmetric.
- It's commonly used to model real-world data like heights, weights, exam scores, and many natural phenomena.

Binomial Distribution
-The binomial distribution is used when you have a series of independent trials, each with only two possible outcomes, such as success or failure.
- It's characterized by two key parameters: the number of trials (experiments) and the probability of success in each trial.

- The binomial distribution is often used to calculate the probability of getting a specific number of successes in a fixed number of trials. For example, you might use it to determine the chances of getting a certain number of heads in a series of coin tosses or the probability of passing a certain number of questions on a multiple-choice test.

These two distributions are fundamental in statistics and are applied in various fields to understand and analyze data. The normal distribution describes continuous data with a symmetric pattern, while the binomial distribution deals with discrete data involving binary outcomes.

Reading Assignment: Introduction to Hypothesis Testing

Hypothesis testing is a fundamental concept in statistics that allows us to make informed decisions based on data. It's a systematic way to evaluate and draw conclusions about a population parameter or a hypothesis.

Key Components of Hypothesis Testing

1. Null Hypothesis (H0): The null hypothesis is a statement or assumption that there is no significant effect, relationship, or difference in the population. It represents the status quo or the default assumption.

2. Alternative Hypothesis (Ha or H1): The alternative hypothesis is the statement that contradicts the null hypothesis. It suggests that there is a significant effect, relationship, or difference in the population.

3. Significance Level (α): The significance level, denoted as α (alpha), is the predetermined level of risk that the researcher is willing to accept to make a Type I error (incorrectly rejecting a true null hypothesis). Common significance levels include 0.05 or 0.01.

4. Test Statistic: The test statistic is a numerical value calculated from the sample data. It measures how far the sample result is from what is expected under the null hypothesis.

5. P-Value: The p-value is a probability value that represents the likelihood of obtaining a test statistic as extreme as, or more extreme than, the one observed, assuming the null hypothesis is true. A smaller p-value suggests stronger evidence against the null hypothesis.

Steps in Hypothesis Testing

1. Formulate Hypotheses: Start by stating the null hypothesis (H0) and the alternative hypothesis (Ha or H1). These hypotheses should be specific and testable.

2. Collect Data: Gather data through experiments, surveys, or observations.

3. Choose a Significance Level (α): Decide on the level of significance that represents the acceptable risk of Type I error. Common choices are 0.05 or 0.01.

4. Calculate the Test Statistic: Compute the test statistic based on the sample data and the chosen test method (e.g., t-test, chi-squared test, z-test).

5. Calculate the P-Value: Determine the probability of observing a test statistic as extreme as the one obtained, assuming the null hypothesis is true.

6. Make a Decision: Compare the p-value to the chosen significance level (α).
    - If $p \leq \alpha$, reject the null hypothesis (evidence against the null hypothesis).
    - If $p > \alpha$, fail to reject the null hypothesis (insufficient evidence to reject).

7. Draw Conclusions: Based on the decision in step 6, draw conclusions and interpret the results in the context of the research question.

8. Report Findings: Clearly communicate the results, including the decision, the p-value, and the implications of the findings.

Hypothesis testing is a critical tool in scientific research, allowing researchers to draw meaningful conclusions from data and make informed decisions. It helps answer questions about the significance of observed effects, relationships, or differences in populations.

Hand-on: statistical examples in Python

Exercise 1 Descriptive Statistics

Calculate mean, median, and standard deviation for a dataset.

Type the following code in a new python script using VSCode and saved in the folder of your choice as file name such as ex1.py and run the script in the terminal:

```python
import numpy as np

data = np.array([25, 28, 30, 32, 35, 38, 40, 45, 50, 55])

mean = np.mean(data)
median = np.median(data)
```

```
std_dev = np.std(data)

print("Mean:", mean)
print("Median:", median)
print("Standard Deviation:", std_dev)
```

Figure 34 terminal output of ex1.py

Exercise 2 Hypothesis Testing

Perform a t-test to compare two sets of data.

Type the following code in a new python script using VSCode and saved in the folder of your choice as file name such as ex2.py and run the script in the terminal:

```
import scipy.stats as stats

data_group_1 = [25, 28, 30, 32, 35]
data_group_2 = [38, 40, 45, 50, 55]

t_statistic, p_value = stats.ttest_ind(data_group_1, data_group_2)

print("T-statistic:", t_statistic)
print("P-value:", p_value)
```

```
if p_value < 0.05:
    print("Reject the null hypothesis")
else:
    print("Fail to reject the null hypothesis")
```

| PROBLEMS | OUTPUT | DEBUG CONSOLE | TERMINAL | PORTS |

```
● PS C:\Users\teokk> cd C:\myproject\day7
● PS C:\myproject\day7> python .\ex2.py
  T-statistic: -4.367161585455664
  P-value: 0.0023895664285419477
  Reject the null hypothesis
○ PS C:\myproject\day7> ▮
```

Figure 35 terminal output of ex2.py

Exercise 3 Data Visualization:

Create histograms and box plots to visualize data distributions.

Type the following code in a new python script using VSCode and saved in the folder of your choice as file name such as ex3.py and run the script in the terminal:

```
import matplotlib.pyplot as plt
import seaborn as sns

data = [25, 28, 30, 32, 35, 38, 40, 45, 50, 55]
```

```
# Create a histogram
plt.hist(data, bins=5, color='skyblue')
plt.xlabel('Value')
plt.ylabel('Frequency')
plt.title('Histogram')
plt.show()

# Create a box plot
sns.boxplot(data=data, color='salmon')
plt.xlabel('Data')
plt.title('Box Plot')
plt.show()
```

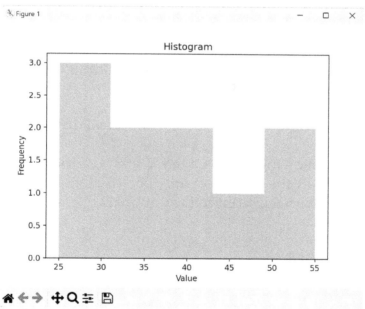

Figure 36 Screenshot of a window displaying the plot. (your plot should be in color)

Exercise 4 Probability Distributions:

Generate random samples from a normal distribution.

Type the following code in a new python script using VSCode and saved in the folder of your choice as file name such as ex4.py and run the script in the terminal:

```
import numpy as np
import matplotlib.pyplot as plt

# Generate random samples from a normal distribution
mu, sigma = 0, 1  # Mean and standard deviation
samples = np.random.normal(mu, sigma, 1000)

# Create a histogram to visualize the distribution
plt.hist(samples, bins=30, density=True, alpha=0.5)
plt.xlabel('Value')
plt.ylabel('Probability')
plt.title('Normal Distribution')
plt.show()
```

Figure 1

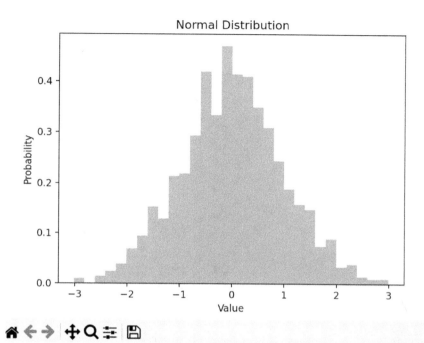

Figure 37 Screenshot of a window displaying the plot. (your plot should be in color)

Day 8: Machine Learning Basics

Day 8: Machine Learning Basics

Day 8: Machine Learning Basics

Reading Assigment: Introduction to Machine Learning

Machine learning is a revolutionary field of artificial intelligence that has transformed the way we solve complex problems and make decisions in various domains. At its core, machine learning is all about enabling computers to learn from data and improve their performance over time without explicit programming. This capability has unlocked new possibilities and opportunities across industries, from healthcare and finance to entertainment and transportation.

In this introduction to machine learning, we will explore the fundamental concepts, techniques, and applications that underpin this dynamic field. Whether you are a novice eager to understand the basics or a professional seeking to deepen your knowledge, this overview will provide you with a solid foundation to embark on your journey into the world of machine learning.

What is Machine Learning?

Machine learning is a subset of artificial intelligence (AI) that focuses on developing algorithms and models capable of learning from data and making predictions or decisions based on that learning. The central idea is to create systems that can identify patterns, generalize from past experiences, and adapt to new information without being explicitly programmed to do so.

Traditional programming relies on a set of predefined rules and instructions to perform tasks. In contrast, machine learning algorithms use data-driven approaches to discover patterns and relationships within the data. These algorithms are designed to improve their performance as they are exposed to more data, making them highly adaptable and capable of handling complex tasks that are difficult to solve with traditional programming methods.

Key Concepts in Machine Learning

To understand machine learning, it's important to grasp some key concepts:

1. Data: Data is the lifeblood of machine learning. It can take many forms, such as text, images, numerical values, or even sound. Machine learning models use data to learn patterns and make predictions.

2. Algorithm: Machine learning algorithms are mathematical and statistical techniques that extract patterns from data. These algorithms vary in complexity and are chosen based on the specific problem being addressed.

3. Training: In the training phase, machine learning models are exposed to labeled data, where the correct outcomes are known. The model learns from this data to make predictions.

4. Testing and Evaluation: After training, the model is tested on new, unseen data to evaluate its performance. Common metrics like accuracy, precision, recall, and F1 score are used to assess model performance.

5. Feature Engineering: Feature engineering involves selecting and transforming relevant data features to improve a model's performance.

6. Supervised, Unsupervised, and Reinforcement Learning: Machine learning can be categorized into different types, including supervised learning (learning from labeled data), unsupervised learning (finding patterns in unlabeled data), and reinforcement learning (learning through interaction with an environment).

Applications of Machine Learning

Machine learning has a wide range of applications, some of which include:

- Natural Language Processing (NLP): Machine learning is used in NLP tasks like language translation, sentiment analysis, and chatbots.

- Computer Vision: It enables image and video analysis for tasks like facial recognition, object detection, and autonomous driving.

- Healthcare: Machine learning aids in disease diagnosis, drug discovery, and patient management.

- Finance: It's used for fraud detection, stock market prediction, and credit risk assessment.

- Recommendation Systems: Machine learning powers recommendation algorithms used by platforms like Netflix and Amazon.

- Robotics: Machine learning is integral to autonomous robots and drones.

- Manufacturing: It optimizes production processes and quality control.

Machine learning is a transformative technology with the potential to revolutionize industries and our daily lives. It empowers computers to learn from data and make intelligent decisions, opening up new possibilities for automation, optimization, and innovation. As you delve deeper into the world of machine learning, you'll discover a diverse array of algorithms, tools, and techniques, each tailored to solve specific types of problems. The journey into this exciting field promises continuous learning and a front-row seat to the future of artificial intelligence.

Reading Assignment: Supervised Learning vs. Unsupervised Learning

Supervised Learning vs. Unsupervised Learning: Understanding the Difference

Machine learning encompasses a diverse set of techniques and approaches, each tailored to specific problem-solving scenarios. Two fundamental branches of machine learning are supervised learning and unsupervised learning. These approaches differ in how they utilize data and the types of problems they are suited to address. In this exploration, we will delve into the key characteristics, applications, and examples of both supervised and unsupervised learning.

Supervised Learning

Supervised learning is a type of machine learning where the algorithm is trained on a labeled dataset. Labeled data consists of input-output pairs, where the input is the data the model observes, and the output is the desired prediction or target. The primary objective of supervised learning is to learn a mapping or function that can accurately predict the output for new, unseen inputs.

Key Characteristics:

1. Labeled Data: Supervised learning requires a dataset in which each data point is associated with a correct target or label.

2. Predictive Modeling: It is used for tasks like classification (assigning data points to predefined categories) and regression (predicting numerical values).

3. Feedback Loop: During training, the algorithm receives feedback in the form of errors or differences between its predictions and the true labels. It adjusts its internal parameters to minimize these errors.

Applications:

- Image Classification: Identifying objects or patterns within images, such as classifying animals in photographs.

- Spam Detection: Distinguishing between spam and legitimate emails.

- Medical Diagnosis: Predicting disease outcomes or identifying anomalies in medical scans.

- Language Translation: Translating text from one language to another.

Unsupervised Learning

Unsupervised learning, on the other hand, deals with unlabeled data. It involves finding patterns, structures, or relationships within the data without explicit guidance or predefined categories. Unlike supervised learning, there are no correct answers or target values to guide the learning process in unsupervised learning.

Key Characteristics:

1. Unlabeled Data: Unsupervised learning operates on datasets without predefined labels or categories.

2. Pattern Discovery: It focuses on discovering hidden patterns, grouping similar data points, or reducing the dimensionality of data.

3. Clustering and Dimensionality Reduction: Common tasks include clustering (grouping similar data points) and dimensionality reduction (simplifying data while retaining essential information).

Applications:

- Customer Segmentation: Identifying groups of customers with similar purchasing behavior.

- Anomaly Detection: Detecting unusual patterns or outliers in data, which can be indicative of fraud or errors.

- Topic Modeling: Grouping similar documents together based on their content.

- Recommendation Systems: Suggesting products or content based on user preferences.

Examples

To illustrate the difference between supervised and unsupervised learning, consider the following examples:

Supervised Learning Example:

Imagine you want to build a spam email filter. You have a dataset of emails, each labeled as either "spam" or "not spam." In supervised learning, you train a model on this labeled data, allowing it to learn the characteristics of spam emails. Once trained, the model can classify new, incoming emails as either spam or not spam.

Unsupervised Learning Example:

Suppose you have a large collection of news articles but don't have any predefined categories or labels. In unsupervised learning, you could apply clustering techniques to group similar articles together based on their content. This could reveal natural categories or topics present in the data, such as sports, politics, or technology.

In summary, supervised learning and unsupervised learning are foundational concepts in machine learning, each serving distinct purposes. Supervised learning excels at predictive tasks with labeled data, while unsupervised learning is ideal for discovering patterns and structures within unlabeled data. These two paradigms, along with other specialized learning approaches, collectively contribute to the power and versatility of machine learning in solving a wide array of real-world problems.

Reading Assignment: Model Evaluation and Validation

Machine learning models are powerful tools for making predictions and decisions based on data. However, their effectiveness and reliability depend on how well they are evaluated and validated. In this discussion, we'll explore the essential concepts and techniques related to model evaluation and validation, highlighting their significance in the field of machine learning.

Why Model Evaluation and Validation Matter

Model evaluation and validation are critical steps in the machine learning workflow for several reasons:

1. Assessing Model Performance: These processes allow us to understand how well a model is performing on unseen data. It helps answer questions like: Is the model accurate? Does it generalize to new data?

2. Comparing Models: Model evaluation helps data scientists and researchers compare different models or algorithms to choose the best one for a given task.

3. Avoiding Overfitting: Validation helps identify and mitigate overfitting, a common problem where a model performs well on training data but poorly on new data.

4. Tuning Hyperparameters: Model evaluation guides the optimization of hyperparameters (settings that control model behavior) to achieve better results.

Key Concepts in Model Evaluation

1. Training Data and Testing Data:

   - Training Data: This is the portion of the dataset used to train the model. The model learns patterns and relationships from this data.

   - Testing Data: This is a separate portion of the dataset that the model has never seen during training. It is used to evaluate the model's performance on new, unseen examples.

2. Metrics for Model Evaluation:

   -Accuracy**: Measures the proportion of correct predictions made by the model.

   - Precision and Recall: Important for imbalanced datasets, precision measures the accuracy of positive predictions, while recall measures the ability to find all positive instances.

   - F1 Score: A combination of precision and recall that balances their trade-off.

   - Mean Absolute Error (MAE) and Mean Squared Error (MSE): Common metrics for regression tasks, quantifying the error between predicted and actual values.

- Area Under the Receiver Operating Characteristic Curve (AUC-ROC): Used for binary classification problems to assess the model's ability to distinguish between classes.

3.Cross-Validation**:

- Cross-validation is a technique that partitions the dataset into multiple subsets. The model is trained and evaluated multiple times, with each subset serving as both training and testing data. This helps obtain a more robust estimate of model performance.

The Model Evaluation Process

1. Data Splitting: The dataset is divided into training and testing sets, typically with a 70-80% portion for training and the remainder for testing.

2. Model Training: The chosen machine learning model is trained on the training data using specific algorithms and settings.

3. Model Testing: The trained model is tested on the testing data, and its performance is measured using relevant evaluation metrics.

4. Validation and Hyperparameter Tuning: If the model's performance is unsatisfactory, it may require adjustments. Hyperparameters like learning rates or tree depths can be fine-tuned to optimize performance.

4. Final Evaluation: Once satisfied with the model's performance on the testing data, it can be considered for deployment to make predictions on new, unseen data.

Overfitting and Underfitting

Overfitting occurs when a model learns the training data too well, capturing noise and irrelevant details. This leads to poor performance on new data. Underfitting, on the other hand, happens when a model is too simple to capture the underlying patterns in the data. Cross-validation and monitoring performance on both training and testing data can help detect and mitigate these issues.

model evaluation and validation are indispensable stages in the machine learning workflow. They ensure that models are reliable, robust, and capable of making accurate predictions on new data. By understanding the principles and techniques involved, data scientists and machine learning practitioners can build models that excel in a wide range of applications, from image recognition to financial forecasting, and contribute to advancements in artificial intelligence.

Hand-on: Machine Learning

Exercise1: Building a simple linear regression machine learning model.

Building a simple machine learning model, such as linear regression, is a great way to get started with machine learning. In this exercise, we'll walk through the steps to build a linear regression model using Python and a sample dataset. Linear regression is a supervised learning technique used for predicting a numerical value (the target) based on one or more input features.

Step 1: Set Up Your Environment

Before you begin, make sure you have Python and the necessary libraries installed. You can use popular libraries like NumPy, pandas, and scikit-learn for this exercise. You can install them using pip if you haven't already:

pip install numpy pandas scikit-learn

Step 2: Load and Explore Your Dataset

For this exercise, let's assume you have a CSV file named "dataset.csv" with two columns: "X" (input feature) and "Y" (target variable). You can use any dataset of your choice.

```
# Load the California Housing Prices dataset
data = fetch_california_housing(as_frame=True)
df = pd.DataFrame(data.data, columns=data.feature_names)
df['Price'] = data.target
```

Step 3: Data Preprocessing

You may need to preprocess your data by handling missing values, scaling features, and splitting it into training and testing sets. For simplicity, we'll assume that the data is clean, and we'll split it into features (X) and the target (Y).

```
X = data[['X']]
Y = data['Y']
```

Step 4: Split the Data into Training and Testing Sets

Split your data into two sets: one for training the model and one for testing its performance. The common split ratio is 70-80% for training and 20-30% for testing.

from sklearn.model_selection import train_test_split

X_train, X_test, Y_train, Y_test = train_test_split(X, Y, test_size=0.2, random_state=42)

Step 5: Build and Train the Linear Regression Model

Now, it's time to create your linear regression model and train it using the training data.

from sklearn.linear_model import LinearRegression

 # Create a Linear Regression model
model = LinearRegression()

 # Train the model on the training data
model.fit(X_train, Y_train)

Step 6: Make Predictions

Once your model is trained, you can use it to make predictions on the testing data.

Y_pred = model.predict(X_test)

Step 7: Evaluate the Model

Evaluate the performance of your model using appropriate evaluation metrics. Common metrics for regression tasks include Mean Absolute Error (MAE), Mean Squared Error (MSE), and R-squared (R2) score.

```
from sklearn.metrics import mean_absolute_error, mean_squared_error, r2_score

mae = mean_absolute_error(Y_test, Y_pred)
mse = mean_squared_error(Y_test, Y_pred)
r2 = r2_score(Y_test, Y_pred)

print("Mean Absolute Error:", mae)
print("Mean Squared Error:", mse)
print("R-squared:", r2)
```

Step 8: Visualize the Results

You can visualize the model's predictions and how they compare to the actual values using libraries like Matplotlib.

```
import matplotlib.pyplot as plt

# Scatter plot for actual vs. predicted prices
plt.figure(figsize=(10, 6))
plt.scatter(y_test, y_pred, alpha=0.5)
plt.xlabel("Actual Prices")
plt.ylabel("Predicted Prices")
plt.title("Actual Prices vs. Predicted Prices")
plt.grid(True)
plt.show()plt.show()
```

The full code listing for exercise 1

```
# Import necessary libraries
import numpy as np
import pandas as pd

import matplotlib.pyplot as plt
from sklearn.datasets import fetch_california_housing
from sklearn.model_selection import train_test_split
from sklearn.linear_model import LinearRegression
from sklearn.metrics import mean_absolute_error, mean_squared_error, r2_score

# Load the California Housing Prices dataset
data = fetch_california_housing(as_frame=True)
df = pd.DataFrame(data.data, columns=data.feature_names)
df['Price'] = data.target

# Split the dataset into features (X) and the target variable (y)
X = df.drop('Price', axis=1)
y = df['Price']
```

```python
# Split the data into training and testing sets (80% training, 20% testing)
X_train, X_test, y_train, y_test = train_test_split(X, y, test_size=0.2, random_state=42)

# Create a Linear Regression model
model = LinearRegression()

# Train the model on the training data
model.fit(X_train, y_train)

# Make predictions on the test data
y_pred = model.predict(X_test)

# Calculate evaluation metrics
mae = mean_absolute_error(y_test, y_pred)
mse = mean_squared_error(y_test, y_pred)
r2 = r2_score(y_test, y_pred)

# Print the evaluation metrics
print("Mean Absolute Error:", mae)
print("Mean Squared Error:", mse)
print("R-squared:", r2)

# Example: Estimate the price of a house with the following features
new_house_features = pd.DataFrame({'MedInc': [4.0], 'HouseAge': [35.0], 'AveRooms': [5.0], 'AveBedrms': [1.0], 'Population': [800], 'AveOccup': [3.0], 'Latitude': [34.1], 'Longitude': [-118.2]})
predicted_price = model.predict(new_house_features)
print("Estimated Price for New House:", predicted_price[0])

# Scatter plot for actual vs. predicted prices
plt.figure(figsize=(10, 6))
plt.scatter(y_test, y_pred, alpha=0.5)
plt.xlabel("Actual Prices")
plt.ylabel("Predicted Prices")
plt.title("Actual Prices vs. Predicted Prices")
plt.grid(True)
plt.show()
```

Run the script and the result as follow:

PROBLEMS   OUTPUT   DEBUG CONSOLE   TERMINAL   PORTS

● PS C:\Users\teokk> cd C:\myproject\day8
○ PS C:\myproject\day8> python .\ex1.py
  Mean Absolute Error: 0.5332001304956563
  Mean Squared Error: 0.5558915986952442
  R-squared: 0.575787706032451
  Estimated Price for New House: 2.2154659725333516

Figure 38 terminal output of ex1.py

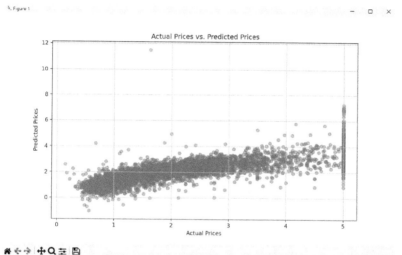

Figure 39 Screenshot of a window displaying the plot.
(your plot should be in color)

The scatter plot you created in your code, comparing actual prices (y_test) with predicted prices (y_pred), is a common visualization used in regression analysis to assess the performance of a predictive model. Here's an explanation of what the scatter plot conveys:

X-Axis (Actual Prices): The values on the x-axis represent the actual target prices of the houses in your test dataset. Each point on the x-axis corresponds to a specific house in the test dataset.

Y-Axis (Predicted Prices): The values on the y-axis represent the predicted prices of the houses by your linear regression model. Each point on the y-axis corresponds to the model's prediction for the respective house in the test dataset.

Data Points: Each point on the scatter plot represents one house from your test dataset. The position of each point is determined by its actual price (x-axis) and the price predicted by your model (y-axis).

Diagonal Line: The diagonal line on the scatter plot represents the ideal scenario where the predicted prices perfectly match the actual prices. In other words, it's the line where y = x. Points that fall exactly on this line indicate that the model's predictions are spot on.

Point Spread: The distribution of points around the diagonal line indicates how well your model is performing. Ideally, you would want the points to cluster closely around the diagonal line. This means that the model's predictions are close to the actual prices. If the points deviate significantly from the line, it suggests that the model's predictions are less accurate.

Scatter Patterns: Patterns in the scatter plot can reveal insights about the model's performance. For example:

Concentrated Points: If the points are closely clustered around the diagonal line, it indicates that the model is making accurate predictions.

Systematic Deviation: If the points form a systematic pattern (e.g., all points are consistently above or below the diagonal line), it suggests that the model has a bias or is making a consistent error.

Scattered Points: If the points are widely scattered without a clear pattern, it may indicate that the model is not capturing the underlying relationships in the data effectively.

In summary, the scatter plot allows you to visually assess how well your linear regression model is performing by comparing its predictions to the actual target values. It helps you identify any systematic errors or patterns in the model's predictions and gives you an intuitive sense of its accuracy.

Day 9: Data Science Projects

Day 9: Data Science Projects

Reading Assignment: Real-world data science projects

Data science has become an integral part of decision-making processes across various industries. Real-world data science projects involve the application of statistical, mathematical, and computational techniques to extract valuable insights, solve complex problems, and drive data-driven decision-making. In this overview, we will delve into the key aspects of real-world data science projects, from problem definition to implementation and communication of results.

1. Problem Definition:
   - Identify a specific business problem or question that can be addressed with data.
   - Define clear objectives and key performance indicators (KPIs) to measure success.
   - Understand domain knowledge and constraints to ensure the problem is solvable.

2. Data Collection:
   - Gather relevant data from various sources, such as databases, APIs, web scraping, or sensors.
   - Ensure data quality by handling missing values, outliers, and inconsistencies.

- Maintain data privacy and security, adhering to relevant regulations.

3. Data Exploration and Preprocessing:
   - Perform exploratory data analysis (EDA) to understand the data's characteristics.
   - Visualize data using charts and graphs to identify patterns and outliers.
   - Preprocess data through techniques like normalization, scaling, and feature engineering.

4. Model Selection:
   - Choose appropriate machine learning or statistical models based on the problem type (classification, regression, clustering, etc.).
   - Split the data into training, validation, and test sets for model evaluation.
   - Experiment with different algorithms and hyperparameters to optimize model performance.

5. Model Training:
   - Train the selected model(s) on the training dataset.
   - Use cross-validation to assess model performance and avoid overfitting.
   - Tune hyperparameters to improve model accuracy and generalization.

6. Model Evaluation:
   - Assess model performance using relevant metrics (accuracy, F1 score, RMSE, etc.).
   - Compare models and select the best-performing one.
   - Validate the model on the test dataset to estimate its real-world performance.

7. Deployment:
   - Deploy the trained model into a production environment, ensuring scalability and reliability.

- Implement monitoring and alerting systems to detect model degradation or drift.
- Develop APIs or interfaces for integration with other systems.

8. Interpretability and Explainability:
- Understand and interpret model predictions, especially for critical decisions.
- Use techniques like feature importance, SHAP values, or LIME to explain model decisions to stakeholders.

9. Communication:
- Translate technical findings into actionable insights for non-technical stakeholders.
- Create compelling data visualizations and reports.
- Present results and recommendations to decision-makers effectively.

10. Maintenance and Iteration:
- Continuously monitor model performance and retrain it as needed with new data.
- Incorporate feedback from users and stakeholders to improve the model.
- Explore opportunities for automation and optimization.

Real-world data science projects are multifaceted endeavors that require a structured approach from problem definition to deployment and beyond. Success in these projects depends on collaboration between data scientists, domain experts, and decision-makers to leverage data-driven insights for better decision-making, improved processes, and a competitive advantage in today's data-driven world.

Selecting a Dataset and Defining a Problem Statement for a Data Science Project

One of the crucial steps in any data science project is selecting an appropriate dataset and defining a clear problem statement. These initial decisions lay the foundation for the entire project. In this guide, we will discuss the key considerations and steps involved in selecting a dataset and formulating a problem statement for your data science endeavor.

1. Identify Your Objective:
   - Begin by understanding the overall goal of your data science project. What problem are you trying to solve, or what question are you seeking to answer?

2. Domain Knowledge:
   - Acquire domain knowledge related to the problem you want to address. Understanding the context is vital for selecting the right dataset and defining the problem accurately.

3. Data Sources:
   - Determine the potential sources of data that may contain relevant information. Common sources include:
      - Publicly available datasets (e.g., Kaggle, UCI Machine Learning Repository).
      - Proprietary data collected by your organization.
      - Data obtained through web scraping, APIs, or sensors.
      - Surveys or questionnaires designed for data collection.

4. Data Quality and Availability:
   - Assess the quality and availability of the data. Consider factors like data completeness, accuracy, timeliness, and whether the data aligns with your problem statement.

5. Data Exploration:
   - Conduct initial data exploration to gain insights into the dataset's content. This helps in understanding the data's structure, its potential limitations, and the feasibility of using it for your project.

6.Problem Statement Formulation:
   - Clearly define your problem statement. It should be specific, measurable, achievable, relevant, and time-bound (SMART). For example:
   - "Predict customer churn in the telecom industry based on historical customer data."
   - "Classify email messages as spam or not spam using natural language processing techniques."

7. Target Variable:
   - Identify the variable you want to predict or analyze. This is often referred to as the target variable or dependent variable. It's what your model or analysis will focus on.

8. Features Selection:
   - Determine the features (independent variables) that are relevant to solving the problem. Feature selection is a critical step in data preparation.

9.Data Size and Scalability:
   - Consider the volume of data required. Depending on your problem, you may need a large dataset, a small dataset, or something in between. Ensure that your dataset is scalable if needed.

10. Ethical and Legal Considerations:
   - Be aware of ethical and legal considerations, especially if your data includes sensitive or personal information. Ensure compliance with data protection regulations.

11. Iterate and Refine:
   - The process of selecting a dataset and defining the problem statement may involve iteration and refinement as you gather more information and insights.

12. Document Everything:
   - Maintain clear documentation of your dataset selection process and problem statement. This documentation is valuable throughout the project's lifecycle.

Selecting a dataset and defining a problem statement are fundamental steps in the data science project lifecycle. A well-defined problem and a suitable dataset will significantly impact the success of your project. Take the time to carefully consider your objectives, data sources, and ethical implications, and ensure that your problem statement is well-formulated and aligns with your project's goals.

Hand-on Exploratory Data Analysis (EDA) for a Retail Store

Exploratory Data Analysis (EDA) for a Retail Store" project using Python. Please refer to Appendices for the code to generate the fake retail sales data in csv format.

Step 1: Data Preparation

```
# Import necessary libraries
import pandas as pd
import numpy as np
import matplotlib.pyplot as plt

# Load the dataset into a Pandas DataFrame
data    =    pd.read_csv('retail_sales_data.csv')        #    Replace
'retail_sales_data.csv' with your dataset file

# Check for missing values, duplicates, and data types
print(data.info())
print(data.isnull().sum())
print(data.duplicated().sum())
```

Step 2: Data Exploration

```
# Calculate summary statistics
summary_stats = data.describe()

# Visualize the distribution of sales and profit
plt.figure(figsize=(12, 6))
plt.subplot(1, 2, 1)
plt.hist(data['Sales'], bins=20, color='skyblue')
plt.title('Sales Distribution')
plt.xlabel('Sales')
```

```
plt.ylabel('Frequency')

plt.subplot(1, 2, 2)
plt.hist(data['Profit'], bins=20, color='lightgreen')
plt.title('Profit Distribution')
plt.xlabel('Profit')
plt.ylabel('Frequency')

plt.show()

# Explore the relationship between sales and profit using a scatter
plot
plt.scatter(data['Sales'], data['Profit'], alpha=0.5)
plt.title('Sales vs. Profit')
plt.xlabel('Sales')
plt.ylabel('Profit')
plt.show()
```

Step 3: Time-Series Analysis**

```
# Convert the date column to datetime format (if it's not already)
data['Date'] = pd.to_datetime(data['Date'])

# Create a time series plot
plt.figure(figsize=(12, 6))
plt.plot(data['Date'], data['Sales'], label='Sales', color='blue')
plt.title('Monthly Sales Trend')
plt.xlabel('Date')
plt.ylabel('Sales')
plt.xticks(rotation=45)
plt.legend()
plt.show()
```

Step 4: Customer Analysis**

```
# Identify the top customers based on total purchase amount
top_customers                 =                 data.groupby('Customer
Name')['Sales'].sum().sort_values(ascending=False).head(10)

# Visualize the top customers
plt.figure(figsize=(10, 5))
top_customers.plot(kind='bar', color='purple')
plt.title('Top 10 Customers by Total Purchase Amount')
```

```
plt.xlabel('Customer Name')
plt.ylabel('Total Purchase Amount')
plt.xticks(rotation=45)
plt.show()
```

Step 5: Product Analysis

```
# Identify the best-selling products and product categories
best_selling_products          =          data.groupby('Product
Name')['Sales'].sum().sort_values(ascending=False).head(10)

# Visualize the best-selling products
plt.figure(figsize=(10, 5))
best_selling_products.plot(kind='bar', color='orange')
plt.title('Top 10 Best-Selling Products')
plt.xlabel('Product Name')
plt.ylabel('Total Sales')
plt.xticks(rotation=45)
plt.show()
```

Step 7: Insights and Recommendations**

Based on the analysis performed in the previous steps, provide insights and recommendations for the retail store. For example:
- Identify peak sales months and plan promotions accordingly.
- Focus on retaining and rewarding top customers to maintain high sales.
- Stock and promote the best-selling products to maximize profits.
- Consider expanding or optimizing stores in regions with high sales potential.

Remember to adapt this solution to your specific dataset and project requirements. The actual dataset and analysis may vary, but this sample solution provides a framework for conducting an EDA for a retail dataset using Python.

Day 10: Advanced Topics and Beyond

Day 10: Advanced Topics and Beyond

Reading Assignment: Deep Learning & NLP

Advanced data science topics like deep learning and natural language processing (NLP) are powerful techniques that leverage the capabilities of artificial intelligence (AI) to solve complex problems and extract valuable insights from data. Let's briefly introduce these topics:

Deep Learning:

Deep learning is a subfield of machine learning that focuses on artificial neural networks, which are inspired by the structure and function of the human brain. Deep learning algorithms are designed to automatically learn patterns and representations from data, making them particularly effective for tasks involving large and complex datasets.

Neural Networks Deep learning models are typically composed of multiple layers of interconnected artificial neurons (nodes). These layers form a neural network. Deep neural networks, with many hidden layers, can model intricate relationships within data.

- Applications OF Deep learning has achieved remarkable success in various applications, including computer vision (e.g., image recognition and object detection), natural language processing (e.g., language translation and sentiment analysis), speech recognition, recommendation systems, and more.

There are popular deep learning frameworks like TensorFlow and PyTorch that facilitate the implementation and training of deep learning models.

Natural Language Processing (NLP)

- **What is NLP:** Natural Language Processing is a field of AI that focuses on the interaction between computers and human language. It enables computers to understand, interpret, and generate human language in a valuable way.

NLP encompasses a wide range of tasks, including:

Text Classification Assigning categories or labels to text documents (e.g., spam detection).

Named Entity Recognition (NER) is for Identifying and categorizing named entities in text (e.g., identifying names of people, organizations, locations).

Sentiment Analysis determine the sentiment or emotion expressed in text (e.g., positive, negative, neutral).

Machine Translation automatically translating text from one language to another (e.g., Google Translate).

Text Generation Creating human-like text, such as chatbots or automatic content generation.

NLP is challenging due to the nuances and complexities of human language, including context, ambiguity, and cultural variations.

-NLP employs various techniques, including tokenization, word embeddings (e.g., Word2Vec, GloVe), recurrent neural networks (RNNs), and transformer models (e.g., BERT, GPT).

NLP is used in chatbots, virtual assistants (e.g., Siri, Alexa), language translation services, sentiment analysis for social media monitoring, and information retrieval systems.

Both deep learning and NLP are active and rapidly evolving fields with a wide range of applications across industries. They have significantly contributed to advancements in AI and data science and continue to drive innovation in areas like healthcare, finance, autonomous systems, and more. Learning these advanced topics can open up exciting opportunities for solving complex real-world problems using data and AI.

Resources for further learning and specialization

Learning Python for data science is a valuable skill, and there are numerous resources available to help you specialize and deepen your knowledge in this field. Here are some recommended resources to consider:

1. Online Courses:
2.
- Platforms like Coursera offer data science specialization tracks, including courses from top universities like Stanford and the University of Michigan.
- *edX: Similar to Coursera, edX provides access to courses from universities and institutions worldwide, with options for data science specialization.
- Udemy: You can find a variety of data science courses and specialization paths on Udemy, often at a lower cost compared to other platforms.

2. Books:
- "Python for Data Analysis" by Wes McKinney: This book focuses on practical data analysis using Python and is a must-read for aspiring data scientists.
- "Hands-On Machine Learning with Scikit-Learn, Keras, and TensorFlow" by Aurélien Géron:** A great resource to dive into machine learning with Python.
- "Data Science for Business" by Foster Provost and Tom Fawcett: This book provides insights into the business side of data science.

3. Online Tutorials and Documentation:**
- Python's official documentation and libraries like Pandas, NumPy, Matplotlib, and Scikit-Learn provide extensive resources and tutorials.

- Websites like Towards Data Science, DataCamp, and Kaggle offer numerous articles and tutorials on data science topics.

4. Specialization Tracks:
   - Consider pursuing a specialization in a specific area of data science, such as machine learning, deep learning, natural language processing, or data engineering.

5. MOOCs (Massive Open Online Courses):
   - Platforms like Fast.ai, Stanford Online, and MIT OpenCourseWare offer data science and machine learning courses for free or at a low cost.

6. Data Science Bootcamps:
   - Join a data science bootcamp like General Assembly, Metis, or Data Science Dojo for immersive learning and hands-on projects.

7. Coding Platforms:
   - LeetCode and HackerRank are excellent platforms for practicing your Python coding skills, including data science-related challenges.

8. YouTube Channels and Podcasts:
   - Channels like Data School, Sentdex, and Corey Schafer offer Python and data science tutorials.
   - Podcasts like "Data Skeptic" and "Not So Standard Deviations" provide insights and discussions on data science topics.

9. Community Involvement:
   - Participate in data science communities on platforms like Reddit (r/datascience), Stack Overflow, and LinkedIn to ask questions and learn from others.

-Follow Python for Data Science: Zero to Hero in 10 Days FB page to access all the exercises code an support from the Author. FB page link https://www.facebook.com/pythonzero2hero

10. **Hands-On Projects:**
   - Apply your knowledge by working on real-world data science projects. Kaggle provides datasets and competitions to practice and learn from others.

11. **Conferences and Meetups:**
   - Attend data science conferences, workshops, and local meetups to network and stay up-to-date with industry trends.

12. **Certifications:**
   - Consider pursuing certifications like the Microsoft Certified: Azure Data Scientist Associate or the Google Data Analytics Professional Certificate to validate your skills.

Remember that data science is a vast field, and specialization can lead to a rewarding career. Choose your path based on your interests and career goals, and don't forget to continuously practice and apply your knowledge through hands-on projects.

Conclusion

Congratulations on completing the 10-day journey from "Python for Data Science: Zero to Hero!" In just a short span of time, you've gained valuable insights into Python and data science fundamentals. Let's recap what you've covered during this exciting learning adventure:

You started with the basics, understanding why Python is essential for data science and installing the necessary tools. You then dove into Python essentials, covering variables, data types, and basic operations, and learned about control structures like conditional statements and loops. Functions, modules, and data structures were explored, setting the stage for more advanced data manipulation with NumPy and data analysis with Pandas.

Your journey continued with data visualization using Matplotlib and a deep dive into statistics, equipping you with the essential tools for making data-driven decisions. You were introduced to the fascinating world of machine learning, building and evaluating your first machine learning model.

But it didn't stop there. You explored real-world data science projects, practicing the skills you've acquired, and learned how to effectively present your findings. Finally, you got a glimpse of advanced data science topics and discovered resources for further learning and specialization.

This marks the start of your thrilling data science journey. Keep in mind that expertise grows through dedicated effort, persistent learning, and hands-on practice. Continue your exploration, experimentation, and the practical application of your newfound knowledge to solve real-world challenges. For ongoing support and connection with like-minded data enthusiasts, consider joining the Python for Data Science: Zero to Hero community on Facebook at facebook.com/pythonzero2hero. Throughout your 10-day adventure, the author will also be available at the FB page to offer online support, ensuring you have a valuable and enriching learning experience.

Thank you for embarking on this journey with us, and we hope your newfound Python and data science skills will serve as a solid foundation for your future endeavors in the exciting field of data science. Keep coding, keep learning, and keep aspiring to be a data science hero!

Appendices

Code to generate retail sales dataset in CSV format

Below is the code to generate afake retail sales dataset in CSV format. Keep in mind that this dataset is for demonstration purposes and does not represent real-world data accurately. You can use it as a starting point for your data analysis projects. Here's how you can create it:

```
import pandas as pd
import random
from faker import Faker

# Initialize Faker for generating fake data
fake = Faker()

# Create an empty DataFrame
data = pd.DataFrame(columns=['Date', 'Customer Name', 'Product Name', 'Sales', 'Profit', 'Region'])

# Generate random sales data for one year
start_date = '2022-01-01'
end_date = '2022-12-31'
date_range = pd.date_range(start_date, end_date)

for _ in range(1000):  # Generate data for 1000 transactions (you can adjust this number)
    date = random.choice(date_range)
    customer_name = fake.name()
    product_name = fake.word()
    sales = round(random.uniform(10, 500), 2)
    profit = round(random.uniform(1, 100), 2)
    region = fake.state()
```

```
    data = data.append({
        'Date': date,
        'Customer Name': customer_name,
        'Product Name': product_name,
        'Sales': sales,
        'Profit': profit,
        'Region': region
    }, ignore_index=True)

# Save the DataFrame to a CSV file
data.to_csv('retail_sales_data.csv', index=False)

print("Retail sales data saved to 'retail_sales_data.csv'")
```

This script generates random sales data for one year, including the date, customer name, product name, sales, profit, and region. It then saves this data to a CSV file named 'retail_sales_data.csv' in the same directory as your Python script. You can adjust the number of transactions and date range to suit your needs.

Note: To run this script, you need to install the `pandas` library for data manipulation and the `faker` library for generating fake data. You can install them using `pip`

www.ingramcontent.com/pod-product-compliance
Lightning Source LLC
LaVergne TN
LVHW052059060326
832903LV00061B/3627